Maximizing Motivation
for Literacy Learning

TEACHING PRACTICES THAT WORK

Diane Lapp and Douglas Fisher, Series Editors
www.guilford.com/d/edu/TPTW_series

Designed specifically for busy teachers who value evidence-based instructional practices, books in this series offer ready-to-implement strategies and tools to promote student engagement, improve teaching and learning across the curriculum, and support the academic growth of all students in our increasingly diverse schools. Written by expert authors with extensive experience in "real-time" classrooms, each concise and accessible volume provides useful explanations and examples to guide instruction, as well as step-by-step methods and reproducible materials, all in a convenient large-size format for ease of photocopying.

35 Strategies for Guiding Readers through Informational Texts
Barbara Moss and Virginia S. Loh

**The Effective Teacher's Guide, Second Edition:
50 Ways to Engage Students and Promote Interactive Learning**
Nancy Frey

**Dare to Differentiate, Third Edition:
Vocabulary Strategies for All Students**
Danny Brassell

**Effective Instruction for English Language Learners:
Supporting Text-Based Comprehension and Communication Skills**
Julie Jacobson, Kelly Johnson, and Diane Lapp

**Transforming Writing Instruction in the Digital Age:
Techniques for Grades 5–12**
Thomas DeVere Wolsey and Dana L. Grisham

**Maximizing Motivation for Literacy Learning:
Grades K–6**
*Barbara A. Marinak, Linda B. Gambrell,
and Susan A. Mazzoni*

Maximizing Motivation for Literacy Learning

Grades K–6

Barbara A. Marinak
Linda B. Gambrell
Susan A. Mazzoni

Series Editors' Note
by Diane Lapp and Douglas Fisher

THE GUILFORD PRESS
New York   London

© 2013 The Guilford Press
A Division of Guilford Publications, Inc.
72 Spring Street, New York, NY 10012
www.guilford.com

Printed in the United States of America

This book is printed on acid-free paper.

Last digit is print number: 9   8   7   6   5   4   3   2   1

Library of Congress Cataloging-in-Publication Data

Marinak, Barbara A., 1957–
    Maximizing motivation for literacy learning : grades K–6 / Barbara A. Marinak,
Linda B. Gambrell, Susan A. Mazzoni.
        p. cm.—(Teaching practices that work)
    Includes bibliographical references and index.
    ISBN 978-1-4625-0751-1 (pbk.)
    1. Language arts (Elementary).   2. Reading comprehension—United
States.   3. Literacy—United States.   4. Motivation in education.   I. Gambrell,
Linda B.   II. Mazzoni, Susan A.   III. Title.
    LB1576.M3777 2013
    372.6—dc23
                                                                            2012018910

To our husbands—Joe, Larry, and David—
for their support and patience

This book would not have been possible without them!

‹‹

About the Authors

Barbara A. Marinak, PhD, is Associate Professor in the School of Education and Human Services at Mount St. Mary's University, where she teaches reading courses. Prior to joining the faculty at Mount St. Mary's, she spent more than two decades in public education, where she held a variety of leadership positions, including reading supervisor, elementary curriculum supervisor, and acting superintendent. Dr. Marinak co-chairs the Response to Intervention (RTI) Task Force of the International Reading Association and serves on the National Joint Commission on Learning Disabilities. Her work has been published in *The Reading Teacher, Literacy Research and Instruction,* and *Young Children.* Along with colleagues Karen A. Costello, Marjorie Y. Lipson, and Mary F. Zolman, Dr. Marinak coauthored a chapter on starting and sustaining a systemic approach to RTI in the 2010 book *Successful Approaches to RTI: Collaborative Practices for Improving K–12 Literacy.* She is also coeditor, with Jacquelynn A. Malloy and Linda B. Gambrell, of another 2010 publication, *Essential Readings on Motivation.* Dr. Marinak's research interests include reading motivation, intervention practices, and the use of informational text.

Linda B. Gambrell, PhD, is Distinguished Professor of Education and former Director of the Eugene T. Moore School of Education at Clemson University, where she teaches graduate and undergraduate literacy courses. Prior to coming to Clemson, she was Associate Dean for Research in the College of Education at the University of Maryland. Dr. Gambrell began her career as an elementary classroom teacher and reading specialist in Prince George's County, Maryland. From 1992 until 1997, she was a principal investigator at the National Reading Research Center at the University of Maryland, where she directed the Literacy Motivation Project. She has served as president of the three leading professional organizations for reading: the

International Reading Association, the National Reading Conference, and the College Reading Association. Dr. Gambrell's major research areas are comprehension and cognitive processing, literacy motivation, and the role of discussion in teaching and learning. Her research has been published in such scholarly journals as *Reading Research Quarterly*, *Educational Psychologist*, *Elementary School Journal*, and *Journal of Educational Research*. Dr. Gambrell is the recipient of professional honors and awards including the College Reading Association's A. B. Herr Award for Outstanding Contributions to the Field of Reading (1994) and Laureate Award (2002), the International Reading Association's Outstanding Teacher Educator in Reading Award (1998) and William S. Gray Citation of Merit (2011), the National Reading Conference's Albert J. Kingston Award (2001), and the Literacy Research Association's Oscar S. Causey Award (2011). She was elected to the Reading Hall of Fame in 2004.

Susan A. Mazzoni, MEd, is an independent literacy consultant who works with administrators and teachers to improve literacy practices in elementary school classrooms. Since the late 1990s, she has worked with teachers on implementing phonics, phonemic awareness, fluency, comprehension, and vocabulary instruction in ways that promote student engagement and literacy motivation. Ms. Mazzoni has taught reading courses and served as a research assistant for the National Reading Research Center at the University of Maryland, College Park. Her research interests include reading motivation, reading engagement, emergent literacy, and discussion. Her work has been published in *The Reading Teacher*, *Reading Psychology*, *Educational Psychology Review*, and *The International Journal of Learning*. In addition, she served as assistant editor and contributing author to the book *Best Practices in Literacy Instruction*.

Series Editors' Note

As our schools continue to grow in linguistic, cultural, and socioeconomic diversity, educators are committed to implementing instruction that supports both individual and collective growth within their classrooms. In tandem with teacher commitment, schools recognize the need to support teacher collaboration on issues related to implementing, evaluating, and expanding instruction to ensure that all students will graduate from high school with the skills needed to succeed in the workforce. Through our work with teachers across the country, we've become aware of the need for books that can be used to support professional collaboration by grade level and subject area. With these teachers' questions in mind, we decided that a series of books was needed that modeled "real-time" teaching and learning within classroom instruction. Thus the series *Teaching Practices That Work* was born.

Books in this series are distinguished by offering instructional examples that have been studied and refined within authentic classroom settings. Each book is written by one or more educators who are well connected to everyday classroom instruction. Because the series editors are themselves classroom teachers as well as professors, each instructional suggestion has been closely scrutinized for its validity.

Maximizing Motivation for Literacy Learning: Grades K–6 opens by engaging readers in the enjoyable task of completing a survey of truth and myth statements, collected by the authors over the years, about nurturing reading engagement. While the survey provides a construct for the topics that are addressed later, it also gives readers an opportunity to analyze their own beliefs about student motivation. Often teachers struggle with ways to move *extrinsic* motivation to *intrinsic* motivation—especially because it seems that the world is driven by extrinsic compensation, and students are easily motivated by rewards like stickers and homework passes.

Acknowledging the truth that extrinsic rewards are where motivation may begin, the authors maximize teachers' understanding of every aspect of motivation by providing instructional examples that reward readers for the intrinsic enjoyment and knowledge gained through reading and sharing a good book. The examples of motivating practices in this book are more than enjoyable; they also are authentic in that they promote the literacy goals fostered through meaningful instruction. The circle of motivated learners grows into a community as students serve as models for each other. Of course, the authors illustrate through their examples that the *first* model is the classroom teacher, whose love of literacy is conveyed through what is read, said, and shared. The community spirit becomes one of literacy pride. Self-regulated, meaningful literacy practices are nurtured with student *choice* as a primary ingredient that spurs ownership and motivation.

We invite you into the "real-time" teaching offered in this book and hope you'll find this series useful as you validate and expand your teaching repertoire. And if you have an idea for a book, please contact us!

DIANE LAPP
DOUGLAS FISHER

Introduction
Myths and Truths

Intrinsic reading motivation is complex. How to effectively nurture intrinsic motivation in young readers has been the subject of research and discussion for several decades. Such scrutiny has yielded important findings and a few misconceptions. To begin our discussion of maximizing reading motivation, we invite you to reflect on some statements by taking the Myths and Truths Survey (see Form 1 on the next page).

The items in the survey were collected from teachers and teacher educators who were asked two questions: What are *myths* related to nurturing intrinsic reading motivation? What are *truths* related to nurturing intrinsic reading motivation? You will notice that the response to each statement could be *myth*, *truth*, or *depends*. *Depends* is a critical option on such a survey because many aspects of nurturing intrinsic motivation will depend on the conditions and contexts in which the action is carried out.

We hope the Myths and Truths Survey provides a framework for you and your colleagues to begin thinking about your practices related to intrinsic reading motivation. Moreover, we suggest the survey is a great way to promote lively discussions in your professional learning community.

Maximizing Motivation for Literacy Learning K–6

> Your work as a teacher of reading is not done
> until you have taught the children three things:
> 1. How to read
> 2. What to read
> 3. To read.
> —AITON (1916, p. 61)

The more you read, the better a reader you become. As with many things in life, practice improves performance. If students are motivated to read, they will choose to

Myths and Truths Survey

Response codes: M = Myth; T = Truth; D = Depends

1. Teachers are critical to nurturing and maintaining reading motivation.	M	T	D
2. Public displays of reading achievement undermine intrinsic motivation.	M	T	D
3. Providing choice nurtures intrinsic reading motivation.	M	T	D
4. Tasks and texts within the zone of proximal development are motivating.	M	T	D
5. Boys are less motivated to read than girls.	M	T	D
6. Extrinsic rewards always lead to intrinsic motivation.	M	T	D
7. Teacher read-alouds are motivating.	M	T	D
8. Struggling readers are generally less motivated to read than proficient readers.	M	T	D
9. Motivation declines as grade levels increase.	M	T	D
10. All students lack the motivation to read complex text.	M	T	D
11. Girls like to read fiction; boys like to read nonfiction.	M	T	D
12. Motivation is an important scaffold when text becomes challenging.	M	T	D
13. Teachers cannot impact the motivation to read.	M	T	D
14. Authentic reading experiences are motivating.	M	T	D
15. Motivation is idiosyncratic.	M	T	D

read. If students choose to read, their reading proficiency will increase. On the other hand, if students are not motivated to read, they will never reach their full literacy potential (Gambrell, 2011). This book is about maximizing literacy motivation in the elementary classroom. We contend that the litmus test for any reading program is the enthusiasm and frequency with which students choose to read.

Why is it so important to maximize literacy motivation? The Program for International Student Assessment (PISA) reveals that across the 64 participating countries, students who were highly motivated to read performed significantly better than students who enjoyed reading the least (Organisation for Economic Co-operation and Development, 2010). In addition, the PISA report indicates that students' motivation to read is a predictor of reading comprehension.

Motivation to read can be defined as the likelihood of choosing to engage in reading (Malloy, Marinak, & Gambrell, 2010). The *engagement perspective* articulates the differences between engaged and disengaged readers and describes the characteristics of motivated or engaged readers (Guthrie & Humenick, 2004; Tracey & Morrow, 2012). Engaged readers are intrinsically motivated to read for a variety of personal goals, are strategic readers, are knowledgeable in their new understandings, and are socially interactive about the reading of text (Gambrell, 2009, 2011).

A number of researchers who have explored motivation to read have grounded their work in the *expectancy–value* theory (Eccles, 1983). This theory posits that students may choose to engage in one activity over another based on how well they expect to do, or their *expectancy*. Perceptions of expectancy are influenced by the students' feelings of competence (or incompetence) in completing a task. Students tend to be more motivated to engage in activities where they feel competent and feel there is some possibility of success. Perceptions of value are influenced by the students' assessment of the value or importance of the activity. Students tend to be motivated to engage in activities that hold some value or importance to them. If we want to create classroom contexts that support motivation, we must nurture students' self-concepts as literacy learners and their appreciation of the value of literacy tasks and activities.

Promoting intrinsic motivation to engage in reading and other literacy tasks should be a high priority in the reading curriculum. In the following section, five general principles of motivation are presented that support literacy motivation.

1 **Maximize the motivational context of the classroom library.** Motivation to read and reading achievement are higher when the classroom library is rich in reading materials and includes books from an array of genres and text types, magazines, the Internet, resource materials, and real-life documents (Guthrie et al., 2007; Kim, 2004; Neuman & Celano, 2001). Increasing the number of books and other reading materials in the classroom will have a positive effect on the amount and quality of the reading experiences of the students. We have become more aware in recent years of the importance of having a balance of high-quality narrative and informational books in the classroom library (Duke, 2000). Providing a rich variety of reading materials communicates the message to students that reading is a worthwhile and valuable activity and sets the stage for students to develop the reading habit.

Researchers and educators caution that while having lots of books in the classroom library is essential, it is not sufficient for improving reading motivation or achievement (Byrnes, 2000; Kim & White, 2008). Access to books also implies that teachers should invite children to read by raising interest and curiosity about books and other materials.

2 **Maximize opportunities for students to engage in sustained reading.** Providing students with time to read during the school day will help them develop the reading habit. One source of students' lack of motivation to read, according to Hiebert (2009), can be traced to an insufficient amount of time spent reading in classrooms. Classrooms where students have opportunities to engage in sustained reading provide the necessary foundation that is essential for supporting students in becoming motivated and proficient readers. Studies have documented the finding that time spent reading is associated with both reading proficiency and motivation to read (Allington & McGill-Franzen, 1993; Mizelle, 1997; Taylor, Frye, & Maruyama, 1990).

Other studies have investigated the effects of time spent reading in school and out of school on reading achievement. Time spent reading in school has been shown to be highly correlated with reading achievement (Taylor et al., 1990). In a subsequent study, Guthrie, Wigfield, Metsala, and Cox (1999) found that the amount of time spent reading in and out of school predicted reading comprehension. Given the evidence that time spent reading, particularly during the school day, is strongly associated with reading proficiency, it is surprising that the amount of time students spend in sustained reading of text during the school day has not increased substantially over the years (Hiebert, 2009).

3 **Maximize opportunities for students to make choices about what they read and how they engage in and complete literacy tasks.** Choice is a powerful force that allows students to take ownership and responsibility for their learning (Rettig & Hendricks, 2000). Research indicates that motivation increases when students have opportunities to make choices about what and how they learn (Jang, Reeve, & Deci, 2010; Skinner & Belmont, 1993). In one study, students who were allowed to choose their homework assignment from a number of acceptable options reported higher intrinsic motivation, felt more competent, and performed better on unit assessments than students who were assigned homework (Patall, Cooper, & Wynn, 2010). The researchers concluded that providing choices is an effective way to support the development of intrinsic motivation.

In a study conducted with fourth-grade students, Guthrie and colleagues (2007) reported that motivation and reading comprehension growth increased when students selected their own books, as compared to having books chosen for them by teachers or other adults. In addition, autonomy was supported when students acquired strategies for choosing books they could read and for finding interesting books, and acquired books for personal ownership. Clearly, students who are allowed to choose their own reading materials are more motivated to read, expend more effort, and gain better understanding of the text (Gambrell, 1996; Guthrie et al., 2007; Schiefele, 1991; Spaulding, 1992).

4 **Maximize opportunities for students to socially interact with others about the texts they are reading.** Social interaction about text includes communication with others, through writing and discussion, about what has been read (Applebee, Langer, Nystrand, & Gamoran, 2003). Social interaction includes talking about books with others, reading together with others, borrowing and sharing books with others, talking about books with peers in class, and sharing writing about books with others (Gutherie, Wigfield, & Von Secker, 2000).

Motivation to read is enhanced through social interactions about text (Turner & Paris, 1995). First, peer comments can pique a student's interest and curiosity. Second, students' observations of their peers' progress may increase their confidence in their own ability to succeed. Third, working with others promotes student engagement. Studies have documented the finding that instruction that incorporates social interaction about text increases students' motivation to read and reading comprehension achievement (Gambrell, Hughes, Calvert, Malloy, & Igo, 2011; Guthrie et al., 2007; Ng, Guthrie, Van Meter, McCann, & Alao, 1998).

5 **Maximize opportunities for students to engage in literacy tasks and activities that are relevant to their lives.** One way to enhance reading motivation and achievement is to help students find value and meaning in classroom reading tasks and activities (Guthrie et al., 2007; Hulleman, Godes, Hendricks, & Harackiewicz, 2010; Purcell-Gates, Duke, & Martineau, 2007). Students become more involved and engaged in comprehending text when they can make connections between the texts they are reading and their personal lives (Deci, 1992; Guthrie et al., 2007). Thus, motivation is enhanced when instructional practices focus on connections between school reading and the personal lives of students. In a recent study conducted by Hulleman and colleagues (2010), students who were asked to write about how material they were learning was relevant to their lives were more motivated and more interested than students who were asked to just write about the material.

The central and most important goal of reading instruction is fostering the love of reading. This goal is an important one because the more a person reads, the better a reader he or she becomes. We want all of our students to become motivated and engaged readers who read for both pleasure and information. Thus, we emphasize the importance of creating a classroom literacy environment that supports students in developing positive self-concepts and an appreciation of the value of reading so that they *choose to read.*

How to Use This Book

Simply put, this book is designed to maximize motivation so that students develop the reading habit. With this goal in mind, we present motivating classroom activities that promote intrinsic literacy motivation. Many of the activities described in the following chapters provide opportunities for the integration of the language arts and include many suggestions for engaging students in listening, speaking, reading, and writing. Part One presents activities designed to enhance the motivational context of the classroom. Part Two focuses on activities designed to support students in developing positive self-concepts as literacy learners. Part Three contains activities designed to help students recognize and appreciate the value of literacy. Each method described in Parts One through Three is subdivided into three sections: (1) a brief overview of the method; (2) a description of how the method focuses on motivation and literacy learning; and (3) a section titled *How It Works*, which offers step-by-step instructions for how to implement the method. Some of the methods include a fourth section, *Extension*, which provides additional tips and ideas for implementation of the method.

In Part Four, you will find a case study in which some of the techniques described in this book were used to improve the intrinsic reading motivation of students in fifth-grade classrooms. Part Five provides two instruments you may use to assess your students' motivation to read and write (specifically, self-concept and value) and an interest inventory. In Part Six, we revisit the Myths and Truths Survey presented in this Introduction.

References

Aiton, G. B. (1916). *Standard reference work for the home, school, and library.* Minneapolis, MN: Welles Brothers.

Allington, R. L., & McGill-Franzen, A. (1993, October 13). What are they to read?: Not all children, Mr. Riley, have easy access to books. *Education Week*, p. 26.

Applebee, A., Langer, J., Nystrand, M., & Gamoran, A. (2003). Discussion-based approaches to developing understanding: Classroom instruction and student performance in middle and high school English. *American Educational Research Journal, 40,* 685–730.

Byrnes, J. P. (2000). Using instructional time effectively. In L. Baker, M. J. Dreher, & J. T. Guthrie (Eds.), *Engaging young readers: Promoting achievement and motivation* (pp. 188–208). New York: Guilford Press.

Deci, E. L. (1992). The relation of interest to the motivation of behavior: A self-determination theory perspective. In A. Renninger, S. Hidi, & A. Krapp (Eds.), *The role of interest in learning and development* (pp. 43–70). Hillsdale, NJ: Erlbaum.

Duke, N. K. (2000). 3.6 minutes per day: The scarcity of informational texts in first grade. *Reading Research Quarterly, 35*(2), 202–225.

Eccles, J. (1983). Expectancies, values, and academic behaviors. In T. Spence (Ed.), *Achievement and achievement motives: Psychological and sociological approaches* (pp. 75–114). San Francisco: Freeman.

Gambrell, L. B. (1996). Creating classroom cultures that foster reading motivation. *The Reading Teacher, 50*(1), 14–25.

Gambrell, L. B. (2009). Creating opportunities to read more so that students read better. In E. H. Hiebert (Ed.), *Reading more, reading better* (pp. 251–266). New York: Guilford Press.

Gambrell, L. B. (2011). Motivation in the school reading curriculum. In T. Rasinski (Ed.), *Developing reading instruction that works* (pp. 41–65). Bloomington, IN: Solution Tree Press.

Gambrell, L. B., Hughes, E., Calvert, W., Malloy, J., & Igo, B. (2011). Authentic reading, writing, and discussion: An exploratory study of a pen pal project. *Elementary School Journal, 112*(2), 234–258.

Guthrie, J. T., Hoa, A. L. W., Wigfield, A., Tonks, S. M., Humenick, N. M., & Littles, E. (2007). Reading motivation and reading comprehension growth in the later elementary years. *Contemporary Educational Psychology, 32*, 282–313.

Guthrie, J. T., & Humenick, N. M. (2004). Motivating students to read: Evidence for classroom practices that increase reading motivation and achievement. In P. McCardle & V. Chabra (Eds.), *The voice of evidence in reading research* (pp. 329–354). Baltimore: Brookes.

Guthrie, J. T., Wigfield, A., Metsala, J. L., & Cox, K. E. (1999). Motivational and cognitive predictors of text comprehension and reading amount. *Scientific Studies of Reading, 3*(3), 231–256.

Guthrie, J. T., Wigfield, A., & Von Secker, C. (2000). Effects of integrated instruction on motivation and strategy use in reading. *Journal of Educational Research, 99*, 232–245.

Hiebert, E. H. (Ed.). (2009). *Reading more, reading better.* New York: Guilford Press.

Hulleman, C. S., Godes, O., Hendricks, B. L., & Harackiewicz, J. M. (2010). Enhancing interest and performance with a utility value intervention. *Journal of Educational Psychology, 102*, 880–895.

Jang, H., Reeve, J., & Deci, E. L. (2010). Engaging students in learning activities: It is not autonomy support or structure but autonomy support and structure. *Journal of Educational Psychology, 102*, 588–600.

Kim, J. S. (2004). Summer reading and the ethnic achievement gap. *Journal of Education for Students Placed at Risk, 9*(2), 169–189.

Kim, J. S., & White, T. G. (2008). Scaffolding voluntary summer reading for children in grades 3 to 5. *Scientific Studies of Reading, 12*(1), 1–23.

Malloy, J., Marinak, B., & Gambrell, L. B. (Eds.). (2010). *Essential readings in motivation.* Newark, DE: International Reading Association.

Mizelle, N. B. (1997). Enhancing young adolescents' motivation for literacy learning. *Middle School Journal, 24*(2), 5–14.

Neuman, S. B., & Celano, D. (2001). Access to print in low-income and middle-income communities: An ecological study in four neighborhoods. *Reading Research Quarterly, 36*(1), 8–26.

Ng, M. M., Guthrie, J. T., Van Meter, P., McCann, A., & Alao, S. (1998). How classroom characteristics influence intrinsic motivations for literacy. *Reading Psychology, 19*, 319–398.

Organisation for Economic Co-operation and Development. (2010). PISA 2009 results: What students know and can do—student performance in reading, mathematics and science (Vol. 1). Retrieved from *www.oecd.org/dataoecd/10/61/48852548.pdf.*

Patall, E. A., Cooper, H., & Wynn, S. R. (2010). The effectiveness and relative importance of choice in the classroom. *Journal of Educational Psychology, 102,* 896–915.

Purcell-Gates, V., Duke, N., & Martineau, J. (2007). Learning to read and write genre-specific text: Roles of authentic experience and explicit teaching. *Reading Research Quarterly, 42,* 8–46.

Rettig, M. K., & Hendricks, C. G. (2000). Factors that influence the book selection process of students with special needs. *Journal of Adolescent and Adult Literacy, 43*(7), 608–618.

Schiefele, U. (1991). Interest, learning, and motivation. *Educational Psychologist, 26*(3), 299–323.

Skinner, E. A., & Belmont, M. J. (1993). Motivation in the classroom: Reciprocal effects of teacher behavior and students engagement across the school year. *Journal of Educational Psychology, 85,* 571–581.

Spaulding, C. L. (1992). The motivation to read and write. In J. W. Irwin & M. A. Doyle (Eds.), *Reading/writing connections: Learning from research* (pp. 177–201). Newark, DE: International Reading Association.

Taylor, B. M., Frye, B. J., & Maruyama, G. M. (1990). Time spent reading and reading growth. *American Educational Research Journal, 27,* 351–362.

Tracey, D. H., & Morrow, L. M. (2012). *Lenses on reading: An introduction to theories and models* (2nd ed.). New York: Guilford Press.

Turner, J., & Paris, S. G. (1995). How literacy tasks influence children's motivation for literacy. *The Reading Teacher, 48*(8), 662–673.

Acknowledgments

Barbara and Susan would like to thank all the teachers and leaders who invited them into their classrooms. In particular, they are grateful to Renee Tobias and Kristin Hoffer from East Hanover Elementary School and Chelton Hunter in the Middletown Area School District. Linda would like to thank the students, teachers, and principals at Calhoun Academy, Clemson Elementary, Hollis Academy, Mount Lebanon Elementary, and Ravenel Elementary in South Carolina, who continue to invite her into their classrooms. Barbara, Linda, and Susan would also like to thank Diane Lapp and Douglas Fisher for conceptualizing this series of books to promote effective literacy practices. We are also grateful to Craig Thomas, Senior Editor at The Guilford Press, for his encouragement. His vision and creativity made our writing process thoroughly enjoyable!

Contents

Contents

PART ONE

Motivating Classroom Communities

You can feel it when you enter the room, hear it in the way students
and teachers relate to one another, and see it in the work that is created.
Everyone in the classroom is engaged in a dance of seeking and sharing
knowledge—they are occupied and involved, inclusive, and responsive.
You feel, as you enter, that you're witnessing a community of literate souls.
—MALLOY, MARINAK, AND GAMBRELL (2010, p. 1)

Have you ever experienced learning in a group, where you valued each other as individuals, felt free to share your ideas, appreciated feedback, and perceived a sense of belonging, mutual respect, and collaboration among the group's members? Creating such a classroom environment is essential to student motivation. It is not the individual student alone whom we must consider when thinking about maximizing motivation in our classrooms.

In Part One, we share with you a number of ideas that you can use to cultivate a motivated, learning community. Each idea has the added benefit of promoting literacy learning: reading, writing, listening, and/or speaking. *Citizen of the Month*, *Class Spirit*, *Star of the Week*, and *Happy Happenings* build positive classroom environments by fostering core values in authentic ways, such as treating others with kindness and consideration, and by instilling a sense of personal and classroom pride. *Lifeline: Past–Present–Future* encourages students to think about and share in a novel way their past and present joys and interests and to use that information to ponder future goals and aspirations. *Read-and-Think Corner* honors and respects students as human beings, who sometimes—like ourselves—need a break to "get away from it all."

One of the keys to building a motivated classroom community is recognizing that you—the teacher—are part of that community and your influence is . . . powerful. With *Book Blessing*, for example, teachers share just a tidbit of interesting information about books in the classroom which, amazingly, motivates students to self-select those books for independent reading. And with *Teacher's Reading Log*, the teacher serves as a literacy role model by inviting students to read his or her thoughts and responses to a variety of texts. This method incorporates the powerful motivators of choice, challenge, and collaboration.

And finally, we offer two methods that you can use to engage your student community in meaningful and motivating literacy practice: *Literacy Centers Plus* (for grade levels K–2) and *Literacy Workshop Plus* (for grade levels 3–6). You may have used centers and workshops in your classroom before, but here you'll find ideas that maximize motivation by infusing multiple core principles of literacy motivation, such as authenticity, access to a wide variety of texts and tasks, engaging hands-on materials, choice, collaboration, challenge, and self-regulation.

Consider This

1 We may frequently miss important motivational aspects of classroom community when we focus solely on the motivation of individual students, for example, whether a particular student seems to enjoy learning, whether or not he or she participates, and so on. How would you describe the tenor of your classroom community? How is it similar or different from the description provided in the opening quote? What are some ways in which teachers can create a positive learning environment?

2 The teacher as literacy role model is a critical component of maximizing literacy motivation in classrooms. How might you share your reading and writing experiences with your students?

3 Consider the following scenario: You walk into a classroom and see bright colors, silver stars hanging from the ceiling, and "motivational" bulletin boards that say "Get into Reading!" and "Aim High!". But you don't see any examples of student work or favorite book titles, and most of the texts sit high on a shelf. Though you have limited information, would you consider this suggestive of a motivated classroom community? Why or why not?

Reference

Malloy, J. A., Marinak, B. A., & Gambrell, L. B. (2010). We hope you dance: Creating a community of literate souls. In J. A. Malloy, B. A. Marinak, & L. B. Gambrell (Eds.), *Essential readings on motivation* (pp. 1–9). Newark, DE: International Reading Association.

Book Blessing

We read books that we know about. We find out about good "reads" when friends tell us about books, when we read book reviews in the newspaper, and in a variety of other ways. We do not go into a bookstore or library and ask the media specialist to help us find a book that we know nothing about. Instead, we tend to search out and read books that we are a bit familiar with. The classroom teacher is a powerful motivator and the Book Blessing technique can significantly increase the number and variety of books that students know about.

Focus on Motivation and Literacy Learning

Book Blessing encourages children to select books to read independently. Children are more likely to read books that they know something about. The Book Blessing technique also adds a bit of spice and variety to the typical teacher read-aloud session. As children engage in self-selected reading, take note of the books they are reading. You may notice that many of the books they've selected are the ones you have "blessed."

Most primary grade teachers read aloud at least one book a day to share good books with young children and illustrate the pleasure of reading—exposing them to approximately 200 books across the school year. By adding Book Blessing once a week, the children in the classroom will be exposed to over 700 books each year! Just think of all the books children will know a little bit about if this technique is used throughout the school year. In the upper elementary grades, it may have a more powerful impact. Many upper elementary teachers read aloud from chapter books each day, taking a week or more to complete just one book. In these classrooms, students would be exposed to approximately 40 books a year. But, if the teacher incorporates Book Blessing, the number of books that students are exposed to swells to over 550!

How It Works

When using the Book Blessing technique, the teacher gathers 10 to 15 books and other reading materials from a range of reading levels, and shares some interesting tidbit of information that will make children want to know the rest of the story. Choose one day a week and set aside 10–20 minutes to devote to sharing books with your students. You will want to select a variety of high-interest books and materials to share with your students. Typically, eight to 12 books can be briefly shared at each Book Blessing session. Here are some things to consider as you select books each week:

1 Include a range of genres. Typically you should have approximately 40% informational texts, 40% narrative or story texts, with the remaining 20% representing such genres as poetry, newspapers, magazines, joke books, and riddle books.

2 Be sure that there are some books that will be appropriate for your lowest-level readers and some that would challenge even the most avid reader.

3 Across all grade levels, balance longer books such as chapter books and "one-sit" books (books that can usually be read in one sitting).

4 Gather the children together and tell them that you have a bag or basket of books that you want to share with them because you think they may want to read some of these books.

5 Then introduce each book briefly, giving the title and author, and perhaps commenting on the topic, cover illustration, or author as you tell about or read "just a little bit" from each book. For example, sometimes just reading the first paragraph of a book is enough to make children want to read the book. Or you might comment that you like all the books by a particular author. If you have read the book yourself, you might want to just tell a few things you remember about the book.

6 Keep in mind that it is not absolutely necessary that you read all these books before sharing them, but you should scan them to find something of interest to share or read to the children.

7 After you have introduced the books, put them on the reading table, in book baskets, or in the classroom library—and watch them disappear.

Citizen of the Month

hom do you admire and respect? This activity engages students in identifying and recognizing adults who are deserving of admiration and respect. Students discuss and nominate adults in their school and the wider community who make contributions that are worthy of recognition as Citizen of the Month. Citizen of the Month provides adult role models for students and deepens their understanding of what behaviors are worthy of admiration.

Focus on Motivation and Literacy Learning

Students need good role models. This activity recognizes individuals who are worthy to serve as role models for students. Through the identification and recognition of these individuals, the character traits and behaviors worthy of emulation come to life. This activity presents a number of opportunities for students to engage in writing activities as they nominate individuals and write letters of appreciation for their contributions to the community.

How It Works

1 The teacher should model the identification of someone who deserves recognition because of his or her good citizenship—for example, someone from the school faculty who volunteers for a charity or someone in the community who performed a heroic deed. During this phase when the activity is being introduced, the teacher should engage the students in a discussion of the qualities that are worthy of our admiration, such as courage, charity, or leadership. The box on page 6 is an example developed by one classroom that lists some of the qualities of a deserving individual.

Criteria for Citizen of the Month Award

General Requirements:

Leadership

Character

Service

- ◆ Even-tempered
- ◆ Thinks of good things to say to others
- ◆ Listens to others
- ◆ Thinks of everyone, not just him- or herself
- ◆ Sense of humor
- ◆ Is him- or herself, doesn't try to be something he or she isn't

2 The teacher provides students with an opportunity to develop a special "award" or "certificate of recognition" to be sent to or presented to the Citizen of the Month. See Figure 2.1 for two examples.

3 Students can nominate individuals to be considered for recognition each month. The students can also create a poster for the classroom or school hallway to show the recipients of the Citizen of the Month Award by month, as seen in the example in Figure 2.2.

4 At the beginning of each month, a special celebration can be planned. The person identified as Citizen of the Month could be invited to the classroom to talk about his or her career, charitable acts, community leadership, or good deeds. The class might plan a special ceremony for the presentation of the award.

Extension

Students can each write individual letters or a whole-class letter may be composed and sent to the Citizen of the Month recipient in appreciation of his or her contributions to the community. If students write individual letters, they can be bound into a book to be presented to the Citizen of the Month, perhaps at the special ceremony to honor the individual.

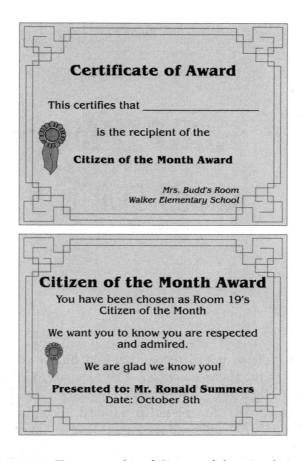

FIGURE 2.1. Two examples of Citizen of the Month Award.

Citizen of the Month Recipients

Mrs. Franks _____   September _____

Mr. Summers _____   October _____

Mrs. Weiss _____   November _____

_____   _____

_____   _____

_____   _____

_____   _____

_____   _____

_____   _____

_____   _____

FIGURE 2.2. Recipient poster for Citizen of the Month Award.

Class Spirit

A Class Spirit bulletin board recognizes and builds positive classroom behaviors. Visitors to the classroom (e.g., other teachers, parents, administrators) are encouraged to look for good things happening in the classroom and to write a "positive comment card" for the bulletin board. As children read the many comments on the Class Spirit bulletin board, their pride in being a member of the class grows and their positive behaviors are reinforced. See Figure 3.1 for an example of a Class Spirit bulletin board.

Focus on Motivation and Literacy Learning

Students are highly motivated to read messages about their own class. Positive comments by others also provide good writing models for the students. This activity encourages reading and writing as well as good behavior. This activity helps to build a classroom culture that focuses on good behavior and promoting classroom values, particularly treating others with kindness.

How It Works

1 The Class Spirit bulletin board can begin when a compliment or positive statement is made about your class. For example, if a fellow teacher happens to mention that your class was especially courteous during a school assembly program or perhaps mentions a very artistic display of student artwork, you could ask that teacher to write a comment card to put on the bulletin board.

2 The Class Spirit bulletin board focuses on behaviors of the class rather than on individual student behaviors in order to build classroom pride and respect.

FIGURE 3.1. Class Spirit bulletin board.

3 Discuss the positive comments with the class, indicating your pleasure and pride at having such a good class!

4 The success of this activity depends on the classroom teacher. The classroom teacher should encourage others to recognize the positive behaviors of the class and to write positive comment cards. For example, a teacher could ask a substitute teacher to leave a positive comment card, or encourage a parent who has visited the classroom to leave one. While a positive comment is not needed every day, encouraging a comment or two a week will keep up the class spirit.

5 It is important that the teacher take the opportunity to talk with the class about the significance of the positive behaviors noted by those who contribute to the bulletin board.

6 Students in the class can also contribute to the Class Spirit bulletin board when they notice good classroom behavior.

Extension

The Class Spirit bulletin board is a dynamic way to recognize the strengths of the class as a whole and to reinforce and build class pride and community. It promotes cooperation, enthusiasm, and communication among class members. When positive behaviors are reinforced, children are more likely to accept greater responsibility for maintaining and enhancing positive class spirit and esprit de corps!

4

Literacy Centers Plus

GRADE LEVELS: K–2

Centers, sometimes called "learning centers" or "stations," involve students working on various tasks within the classroom, with each center or station having its own set of directions and materials (Harris & Hodges, 1995). In Literacy Centers Plus, motivation plays a central role in center planning, as students engage in meaningful, authentic, on-task practice reading, writing, listening, and speaking. Literacy Centers Plus is particularly appropriate for use during small-group instruction time. Students who are not with the teacher can work on these activities by themselves or with a partner, when appropriate.

Focus on Motivation and Literacy Learning

Literacy Centers Plus infuses principles of literacy motivation within each literacy center, including authenticity, access to a wide variety of texts and tasks, engaging hands-on materials, self-selection, limited choice, collaboration and social learning, and appropriate challenge. Literacy Centers Plus promotes a sense of competence and independence as students engage in self-regulated practice of meaningful literacy tasks with peers.

How It Works

1 Create areas in your classroom large enough to occupy three or four students. Too many students at a center can hinder on-task focus. If furniture isn't available or if space is limited, consider using carpet squares for seating and to establish a

niche, or sense of boundary, for each center. We recommend that primary students move from center to center within the classroom, which allows an age-appropriate "stretch break" between center activities.

2 Designate centers and design activities that involve meaningful practice in reading, writing, listening, and speaking. There are many possibilities for engaging literacy centers. We suggest including the following five in your literacy center repertoire:

- ◆ **Library Center** is where students choose texts from the classroom library for independent, self-selected silent reading or buddy reading. Be sure to feature texts at the library center that were used for teacher read-alouds, as students will frequently self-select these texts for rereading (see *Book Blessing* [Chapter 1]). Also, include a variety of genres and text types, including magazines, comic books, poetry, and nonfiction texts to accommodate and stimulate a wide range of student interest. You may organize texts by difficulty at the library center so that students can easily locate reading for independent practice and teach students a way to identify texts that are "just right" in terms of difficulty (e.g., see *High Five* [Chapter 13]). However, we recommend that students have unlimited access to texts at the library center in order to encourage exploration, self-direction, and intrinsic motivation.

- ◆ **Browsing Box Center** (Fountas & Pinnell, 1996) is a leveled text center, where—unlike the library center—students are only offered books within their zone of proximal development. There are frequently four or five boxes of books at this center—one box for each group of students. The boxes may be color-coded or labeled with students' names. Each box contains instructional-level books previously taught and books that are easy to read (independent level) for each group. This center not only fosters reading fluency, it builds students' self-concept and competence as a reader.

- ◆ **Writing Center** involves students writing for varied and authentic purposes, including responding to text, writing about meaningful experiences, report writing, writing to a pen pal, and the like. Include a range of engaging materials at this center, such as blank books for story or report writing; various types of papers, markers, and crayons; and envelopes. Consider providing students with two or three topic choices for writing (limited choice) in order to foster self-direction and intrinsic motivation. Note that when students are asked to "write about anything they want," this can be more challenging than choosing among a short list of generated topics. Writing centers are self-differentiating, as students will necessarily write at their own level. Be sure to praise young children's early attempts, which may include only drawing or scribble writing.

- ◆ **Word Study Center** is where students work with letters and words using a variety of hands-on activities, games, and motivating materials that foster engaged learning. Consider using letter tiles for making words, words or pictures on index cards for sorting (see *Word Sorting for Younger Students*

[Chapter 18]), letter stamps, sight-word rings, phonics games, and so on. The possibilities are limitless. To maximize motivation at this center, we recommend (a) limiting choice of activities to two or three, as too many activities and materials can be overwhelming and impede engagement; (b) using at least some words from students' reading to promote learning transfer, authenticity, and value of reading; (c) differentiating activities among students to afford an appropriate degree of challenge; and (d) including some activities that result in a "product" (e.g., a paper to give to the teacher) for assessment purposes and to instill a sense of student accountability.

◆ **Listening Center** involves students listening to books on CD or tape, preferably using headphones so as not to interrupt children working at other centers. Students benefit from listening to a book at the listening center, regardless of whether or not they have a copy of the book to follow along. Also, primary students enjoy demonstrating competence concerning CD or tape player operations. Once again, consider using limited choice of CDs/tapes to two or three at a time. You may wish to include a product at this center (e.g., a story map) for assessment and accountability purposes.

3 Encourage on-task conversation at centers. Literacy learning involves practice reading, writing, listening, and speaking. Center time provides authentic opportunities for students to speak and collaborate with peers on center activities. Be sure to model and discuss on- and off-task conversations, as well as how to behave with kindness and good manners at centers. Teaching students how to speak at volumes that do not interrupt others is also key to successful center conversations.

4 There is a difference between "fun activities" and "authentic, engaging activities." For example, primary students may have fun coloring a Dr. Seuss character at the writing center, but coloring, generally speaking, is not a literacy activity. Drawing, however, is more like writing in that it involves a representation of ideas. Make sure your activities stimulate both hands-on and minds-on literacy practice!

5 Teach your students how to work at centers. Many teachers use centers when working with a small group of students—that is, centers are what "the other students do" when they are not with the teacher. Consequently, centers can provide students with a sense of independence and self-competence as they work without teacher guidance. However, if students do not have a clear understanding of center behavior expectations, they will tend to exhibit off-task behavior. Consider the fine points when teaching center expectations: desired voice level, what students should do if they have a question or need to use the bathroom, how to share a book, what to do if you can't spell a word at the writing center, how to clean up after using each center, and so on. Use a gradual release model to teach center expectations, where you model desired behaviors and cogenerate a list of expectations for each center. Students then practice with teacher and/or student feedback, and individual students may then "qualify" at each center before being allowed to work "officially" at that center.

6 If possible, teachers should use the same center management systems across K–2. To do this, teachers would need to get together to agree on the same system. A center management system informs students about which centers they can attend and when and how students move from center to center (self-paced or teacher controlled), how many students are allowed at each center, and so on. There are many effective center management systems available to teachers, but we recommend using the same system across K–2 so that primary students don't need to learn a new system at the beginning of each school year. By doing this, you're developing students' self-competence at centers, and returning students are excited to see that they're starting the school year knowing "how to do centers"! Students will find these familiar routines motivating. Center management sameness across K–2 has the added advantage of getting centers up and running quickly at the beginning of the school year so that the focus is on instruction—not retraining students in center management.

References

Fountas, I. C., & Pinnell, G. S. (1996). *Guided reading: Good first teaching for all children.* Portsmouth, NH: Heinemann.

Harris, T. L., & Hodges, R. E. (Eds.). (1995). *The literacy dictionary: The vocabulary of reading and writing.* Newark, DE: International Reading Association.

5

Literacy Workshop Plus

GRADE LEVELS: 3+

In Literacy Workshop Plus, students engage in meaningful, independent literacy activities. We suggest using Literacy Workshop Plus in grades 3–6 in lieu of Literacy Centers Plus (for grades K–2) because students at these levels do not need to move among centers to sustain focus for an extended period of time. Like Literacy Centers Plus, Literacy Workshop Plus is an effective and motivating option when your students need to engage in literacy practice while you meet with small groups. Students who are not with the teacher can work on these activities by themselves or with a partner, when appropriate.

Focus on Motivation and Literacy Learning

Literacy Workshop Plus infuses principles of literacy motivation, including authenticity, access to a wide variety of texts and tasks, self-selection, appropriate challenge, and social learning. Literacy Workshop Plus promotes a sense of competence and independence as students engage in the self-regulated practice of meaningful literacy tasks. The tasks involve important and varied components of literacy, such as generating questions about text, answering questions that require lower- and higher-level thinking, word sorting, responding to text in multiple ways, and silent reading.

How It Works

Consider the amount of time that your students will work independently and arrange a Literacy Workshop Plus containing authentic and meaningful activities. Write the list of activities on the board or chart paper for your students to follow. Consider the following options when building your workshop:

◆ **Q-Matrix.** Asking questions about text is an important comprehension strategy. Also, when students carefully attend to the wording of their questions, they are more likely to comprehend questions posed to them. Q-Matrix (Wiederhold, 1998) is a grid that provides question stems to help students write questions about text. See Figure 5.1.

The Q-Matrix stems are arranged in a cognitive hierarchy. Stems 1–12 can generate literal questions, Stems 13–24 can generate inferential questions, and Stems 25–36 can generate extended questions. Students will need lots of teacher modeling and guided practice before using the Q-Matrix to generate questions independently.

In some cases, you will need to pull the words in a stem apart (Marinak, Mazzoni, & Gambrell, 2012). For example, you might use Stem 15, *Which can*, to generate this question: <u>*Which* bird *can* fly the fastest?</u> Students will need lots of modeling and guided practice before they're able to do this independently.

Students should have their own copy of the Q-Matrix and text for question writing. Students write one, two, or three questions during workshop time. The full Q-Matrix might seem overwhelming to some readers. It may be used more selectively by allowing students to choose one stem or several stems for a reading selection. And for more challenge, assign a row or column of stems. After students write their question(s), prompt students to answer their own and each others' questions during small-group instruction time. Encourage them to look back in text and cite evidence to support their answer.

1. What is/was? What are?	2. Where/When is/was? Where/When are?	3. Which is/was? Which are?	4. Who is/was? Who are?	5. Why is/was? Why are?	6. How is/was? How are?
7. What do? What does? What did?	8. Where/When do? Where/When does? Where/When did?	9. Which do? Which does? Which did?	10. Who do? Who does? Who did?	11. Why do? Why does? Why did?	12. How do? How does? How did?
13. What can?	14. Where/When can?	15. Which can?	16. Who can?	17. Why can?	18. How can?
19. What could/ should?	20. Where/When could/ should?	21. Which could/ should?	22. Who could/ should?	23. Why could/ should?	24. How could/ should?
25. What will?	26. Where/When will?	27. Which will?	28. Who will?	29. Why will?	30. How will?
31. How might?	32. Where/When might?	33. Which might?	34. Who might?	35. Why might?	36. How might?

FIGURE 5.1. Q-Matrix. The Q-Matrix has been copied with permission from Kagan Publishing & Professional Development from the following book: Wiederhold, C. W. (in consultation with Spencer Kagan). *Cooperative Learning & Higher Level Thinking: The Q-Matrix.* San Clemente, CA: Kagan Publishing, 1998. (800) 933-2667. *www.KaganOnline.com.*

◆ **Guiding Questions** (Marinak, Mazzoni, & Gambrell, 2012). Create a series of six to eight questions that, when asked, move students from the beginning of the chapter or book to the end of the chapter or book. Be sure to include some literal, inferential, and extended questions. Pose the questions at the beginning of Literacy Workshop Plus, prior to reading. Clarify questions as needed. Instead of students writing answers to questions, provide students with sticky notes; students place the sticky notes at the beginning of the paragraphs that provide support for the answers. We suggest using sticky notes for Guiding Questions because writing answers to questions can become tedious and even cause children to dislike the book! The use of sticky notes is a more authentic way to prepare for group discussions. Students can label the sticky notes #1, #2, and so on to correspond with the question number. Tell students to be prepared to "answer each question in your own words" and then to "read the paragraph that provides support for your answer" after the workshop. When students read aloud in small groups for the purpose of supporting their answer, this provides an authentic purpose for rereading. Rereading can build reading fluency, and the teacher can also assess how well the student is decoding and comprehending at this time.

  Consider using the Q-Matrix to write Guiding Questions. Use Stems 1–12 to generate some literal questions, Stems 13–24 to generate some inferential questions, and Stems 25–36 to generate some extended questions. This can help you pose questions that offer a range of cognitive challenge.

◆ **Word Sorting.** See *Word Sorting for Older Students* (Chapter 19).

◆ **Teacher's Reading Log.** See *Teacher's Reading Log* (Chapter 8). Workshop time provides an excellent opportunity for students to read your responses to text.

◆ **Research/Presentations.** During Workshop, students may work on research projects (see *Experts Teaching* [Chapter 11], *Make a Real-World Connection* [Chapter 24], and *I-Search* [Chapter 25]) and prepare reports or presentations. Presentations may include oral reports, PowerPoint, posts, maps, charts, graphs, poems, iMovies, blogs, and more.

◆ **Self-Selected Silent Reading.** Some schools provide a sustained silent reading time when the entire class or school "drops everything and reads." Many classroom schedules are so full that there isn't time in the day do this. Workshop is an appropriate time for self-selected silent reading. (Note that unlike "drop everything and read," not all students read independently at the same time during Workshop.) One advantage of including self-selected, silent reading during Workshop is that students will never run out of things to do while you work with a small group. Self-selected silent reading is so important to reading growth and motivation that we suggest that you include this activity in every Workshop. And even if you have a "drop everything and read" time in your schedule, additional self-selected, silent reading will only benefit your students!

Extension

You will foster students' comprehension of text when you include a number of ways to read, reread, and respond. Using a single text (chapter or book), students may, for example, engage in Guiding Questions, Q-Matrix, and Word Sort (include words from the book), and read the Teacher's Response Log about the text.

References

Marinak, B. A., Mazzoni, S. A., & Gambrell, L. B. (2012). *Reaching all readers: Strategic reading intervention: Levels AA-S*. Columbus, OH: Zaner-Bloser.

Wiederhold, C. W. (in consultation with Kagan, S.). (1998). *Cooperative learning and higher-level thinking: The Q-Matrix*. San Clemente, CA: Kagan Publishing.

6

Read-and-Think Corner

A Read-and-Think Corner in the classroom can provide a place for children to "get away from it all." There are times when we all need to have a few minutes alone to collect our thoughts, organize our work, or to simply relax.

A Read-and-Think Corner can be set up in any nook or cranny in the classroom. Make it pleasant and comfortable—find an old easy chair or a rocking chair, or some pillows and a small rug. There should be lots of reading material, a timer of some kind, and possibly some low bookcases to provide a cozy space.

Focus on Motivation and Literacy Learning

Through the use of the Read-and-Think Corner, you can provide opportunities for children to focus on their strengths as they make decisions about how they spend their time, reorganize and plan their work, and/or remove themselves from frustrating or boring situations in a productive manner.

For children, the Read-and-Think Corner can be a haven in the classroom. It can provide a place for calming down, relaxing, or thinking about important things. One child commented, "The Read-and Think Corner gives me a chance to get myself straightened out. . . . I just sit and read a while."

How It Works

1 Children can go to the Read-and-Think Corner whenever they choose—even during teacher instruction. All children have times when they become bored or frustrated during instruction. Instead of distracting or disrupting the group or simply daydreaming, the child can choose to go to the Read-and-Think Corner to read a favorite book or to just sit and think. If a child has a disagreement with a classmate, instead of losing his or her temper or getting into a fight with the other child, the child can go to the Read-and-Think Corner to think things over and cool off. The Read-and-Think Corner provides children with a way to remove themselves from unpleasant classroom situations whenever there is a need. The Read-and-Think Corner is NOT a place where students are "sent" by the teacher. Rather, the Read-and-Think Corner is a place where children can choose to go at anytime they feel the need. Such decision-making opportunities help children learn to be in control of their own behavior. It also supports children in seeing the value of reading for pleasure and relaxation.

2 In the beginning, it might be advantageous to establish a time limit of 5–10 minutes, depending on the age of your students. A sand timer is quiet and easy for younger children to use. Older children may prefer a clock in the Read-and-Think Corner and a sign-in and sign-out sheet on which they write their time of arrival and time of leaving. You will find that this procedure isn't needed for very long, as children will learn to respect the privilege of going to the Read-and-Think Corner.

3 While the children should be allowed to choose whether they use the corner for reading or for thinking, you can encourage reading by making many high-interest reading materials available—for example, magazines, graphic novels, comics, and books.

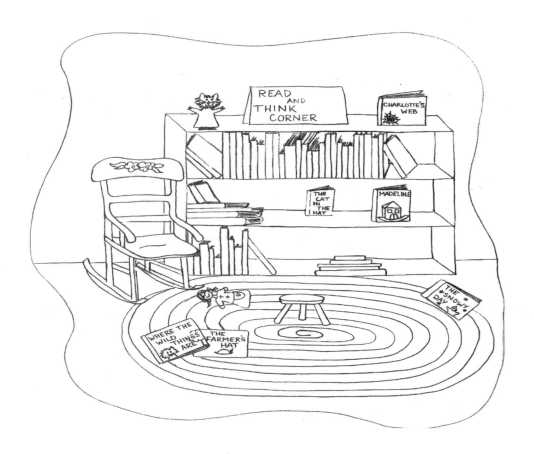

4 Teachers report that the Read-and-Think Corner provides them with interesting and useful information about their students—for example, noticing that a particular child goes to the Read-and-Think Corner frequently during math. The child's reason for going to the Read-and-Think Corner is a private matter and while you would never ask why the child always goes during math, you might be able to determine the reason the child appears to be avoiding the subject. You can then use this information to change the instructional situation to make it more interesting and appealing to the child.

5 If it becomes apparent that a child is abusing the privilege of using the Read-and-Think Corner by spending too much time there, you should have a private conference with the child to determine some possible causes. Perhaps the child is avoiding something—an annoying classmate, a frustrating task, written work, or something less obvious. This is valuable information for the teacher to have in order to develop an intervention to support the child's learning.

7

Star of the Week

Star of the Week focuses on developing children's personal and academic strengths and can foster perceived self-confidence and competence. It provides children with positive feedback and it encourages classmates to look for good things about their peers and to read and write about them.

Focus on Motivation and Literacy Learning

We all like to hear positive things about ourselves. Children are highly motivated to read the good comments written about them by their classmates. Classmates are also interested in reading what other classmates have written about the Star of the Week. This activity encourages student reading and writing for an authentic purpose: the creation of the Star of the Week bulletin board (see Figure 7.1).

When students with low self-concept get positive feedback, it enhances their self-concept and feelings of competence. Star of the Week can have a tremendous impact on the culture of the classroom. It encourages children to look for the good in others. It fosters appreciation of others and illustrates to children that they are valued and respected by their peers. Children get excited about Star of the Week—they look forward to it! In one classroom a child commented, "I can't wait to be Star of the Week to find out what's good about me!"

How It Works

1 Each week, a child's name is picked out of a hat or jar. A better option is to select a boy and a girl for Star of the Week so you would need to have the names of

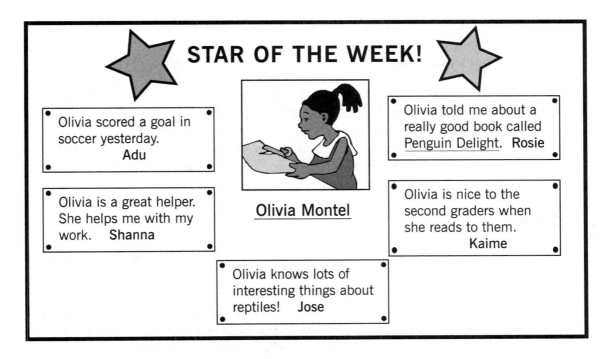

FIGURE 7.1. Star of the Week bulletin board.

the girls in one jar and the names of the boys in another jar. This would allow every boy and girl an opportunity to be Star of the Week over a 3-month period, assuming there are approximately 30 children in the class. The process can then start again. In most classrooms the cycle could be repeated two or three times across the 9-month academic year giving every child the opportunity to be Star of the Week at least two or three times during the year.

2 The child's picture and name are posted on the Star of the Week bulletin board on Monday.

3 The teacher serves as a role model for the class by writing the first positive comment about the child on an index card. The card is then posted on the board. The teacher explains that it is everyone's responsibility to look for the good in others. The teacher might say something like "This week our Stars of the Week are Miguel and Olivia. I want you to think about something you can say about Miguel and Olivia—only positive comments go on our Star of the Week bulletin board. Comments should be honest and positive—there are good qualities in all of us. We always take responsibility for what we say about others so we always sign our names."

4 Classmates are then given a special time to write their comments about the personalities of the week and sign their names. The teacher can work with students to proof spelling and grammar because this is a public board that will be read by anyone coming into the classroom. Student writing should be done in pencil so that corrections can be made easily.

5 The comment cards are then collected by the teacher and posted on the bulletin board. The teacher should again do a general proofing to assure that only positive comments go on the board. Every child in the classroom should contribute to each bulletin board. Reinforce the idea that everyone has good qualities and positive traits—and it is our responsibility to look for and identify good things about others.

Extension

Star of the Week loses its effectiveness when an entire bulletin board is covered with very general comments like "Jonas is nice." Though general comments such as this are positive, children easily and rightly understand the idea that general comments are not as meaningful as specific comments. The teacher can provide some direction for writing more meaningful comments by putting some "general" comments on the board along with some "specific" comments. Students can then be asked to identify the comments that are general and those that are specific. The teacher can then lead a discussion with the class posing questions such as "Which comments really tell a person what is positive?" or "Which comments would you like to hear?".

Another way to help students write more specific comments is to build on what they do write. For example, if a child writes "Jonas is a nice boy," you might ask the child, "Why do you think Jonas is a nice boy? Could you write about some of the things he does that you think are nice?" The comment that "Jonas is nice because he helps me practice basketball" lets Jonas know what he is doing that is appreciated—and specific, positive behavior is reinforced.

Index cards or strips of "positive comment paper" are more useful and efficient than having students try to write directly on the bulletin board for obvious reasons. Students often need to edit their writing before public display. This procedure also allows the teacher to monitor the bulletin board display so that no child is ever embarrassed by a negative or thoughtless comment. Sometimes an inappropriate comment needs only slight editing. You might ask the child to reconsider his or her comment or decide what would make it more positive. For example, if a child wrote "Olivia has pretty eyes; I like her better without her glasses," the teacher might ask the child, "What part of your comment will Olivia really like?" And then discuss how describing Olivia's pretty eyes would be very positive, resulting in a comment such as the following: "Olivia has pretty blue eyes that sparkle when she laughs."

You can involve parents in this activity as well. You can notify parents that their child is the Star of the Week and invite them to write a short note about something the child does at home that is deserving of praise. The parent note or notes can then be posted on the bulletin board.

At the end of the week, the child or children who have been the Star(s) of the Week can take their positive comment cards home. Children like to read these comment cards over and over again and they like to share them with family and friends. There are several ways this can be done. The teacher could take the photo of the child and paste it on an envelope that contains all the comments and give it to the child. Another option is to make a booklet by pasting the child's photo on the cover and then taping or pasting a comment on each page.

8

Teacher's Reading Log

Teacher's Reading Log invites readers into your thinking about text. Maintaining a Teacher's Reading Log makes your metacognition public and allows you to model the wide variety of ways we respond to text.

Focus on Motivation and Literacy Learning

Teacher's Reading Log provides students with an important choice: to read the opinions, thoughts, and responses from you, their teacher. If students choose to read your log, they can be challenged to think about text in new and different ways. They can also collaborate with their peers about books, magazines, and/or newspapers being read by their teacher. Teacher's Reading Log helps create a motivating classroom context.

How It Works

1 Tell students that you will be keeping a reading log. Explain that the log will be available for them to read, if they so choose.

2 Use your log to model responding to all types of text. You might respond to the teacher read-aloud, content material, and/or text being used for reading instruction.

3 Create responses that challenge the thinking of your students. Pose questions. Wonder aloud in your log. Disagree with an author's point of view. Admit to confusions. Explain how text can help reconcile ambiguities.

4 Use a variety of options to represent your responding. This might include numbers, pictures, graphics, cartoons, speech bubbles, and so on.

5 Use your log to model responding across texts. Write about how a text reminds you of other books, magazines, or newspaper articles you have read.

6 After offering a Teacher's Reading Log, enjoy the conversations your children have about your reading!

7 Examples of several Teachers' Reading Log entries are provided on page 28.

Extension

Consider using a Teacher's Reading Log to invite students into text. Pose an interesting question and suggest that the answer to the question might be found in a particular piece of text. Or share a fun-filled or quirky fact and where you found the fact. Remind yourself (and your readers) that more interesting facts can be found in that same text.

Use a Teacher's Reading Log to help children evaluate text and learn their likes and dislikes. Model that we don't, and should not be expected to, like every book or article we read. Explain in your log that you did not like a particular text and explain, with specificity, why you did not care for the book or article. Your preferences are sure to be the subject of many wonderful discussions!

If children have access to the Internet, a Teacher's Reading Log can be maintained via a blog or wiki.

References

Buckley, C. (2009). *Tarra and Bella: The elephant and dog who became best friends.* New York: Putnam.

Collier, J., & Collier, C. (2005). *My brother Sam is dead.* New York: Scholastic.

Dennis, B., Larson, K., & Nethery, M. (2009). *Nubs: The true story of a mutt, a marine, and a miracle.* New York: Little, Brown.

Rylant, C. (2007). *Gooseberry Park.* New York: Sandpiper.

Sattler, H. (1998). *The book of North American owls.* New York: Sandpiper.

Simon, S. (2001). *Tornadoes.* New York: HarperCollins.

Example Entries from Teachers' Reading Logs

Teacher's Reading Log response to *Gooseberry Park* by Cynthia Rylant:

> Gosh, I wonder how many babies Stumpy [the squirrel] will have. What do you think her nest looks like?

Teacher's Reading Log response to *The Book of North American Owls* by Helen Sattler:

> My favorite owl, the snowy owl, has a wingspan of 54–56 inches. That is over 4 feet from tip to tip. Which owl is your favorite and why?

Teacher's Reading Log response to *Tarra & Bella: The Elephant and Dog Who Became Best Friends:*

> Tarra and Bella remind me of Nubs and Brian in *Nubs: The True Story of a Mutt, a Marine, and a Miracle*. These two books are about friendships. Animals like Tarra the elephant and Bella the dog can be friends. Friendship also happens between animals and people like Nubs and Major Brian.

Teacher's Reading Log response to *Tornadoes* by Seymour Simon:

> This book is fascinating and frightening at the same time. I learned from *Tornadoes* that the United States has had two F5 tornadoes. One was in Missouri in 1925 and the other was in Texas in 1997. However, *Tornadoes* was published in 1999. I learned from *weather.com* that since 1999, the U.S. has had another F5 tornado. In 2011, an F5 tornado hit Joplin, Missouri.

Teacher's Reading Log response to *My Brother Sam Is Dead* by James Collier:

> Well, I started this book and I may not be able to finish it. The graphic scenes of Revolutionary War battles are making me uncomfortable.

9

Happy Happenings Box

Students should be encouraged to look for examples of kindness and consideration that occur in the classroom. A Happy Happenings Box in the classroom can serve as a vehicle to help students develop an appreciation for good behavior. As one teacher described the Happy Happenings Box to her class, she emphasized that "We all need to look for the 'good' in others."

Focus on Motivation and Literacy Learning

Students are encouraged to look for happy happenings in the classroom and to write a message, acknowledging the person and the good deed. Students engage in writing for contributions to the Happy Happenings Box and, after the teacher has shared the comments with the class, they can be posted on a bulletin board. Students are always highly motivated to read comments about themselves and their peers.

How It Works

Create a box with a slit in the top and the wording "Happy Happenings Box" on the side (see Figure 9.1). The box does not have to be fancy. Leave it in the classroom for a day or so without telling the students about it—this will build curiosity and interest. If students ask about the box, say something like, "We'll all find out about the box on Friday. What do you think it is for?"

1 The teacher explains that it is important to acknowledge the many good behaviors in the classroom—and that happy happenings occur all the time. It is our responsibility to look for good things in others.

FIGURE 9.1. Happy Happenings Box.

2 The teacher then models identification of a good behavior, such as the class members quickly lining up after recess. The teacher demonstrates how she would write about this Happy Happening on an index card and sign her name. It is important to talk about and illustrate that contributions to the Happy Happenings Box have two parts: first, identification of the good behavior and, second, why it is important. In the following teacher example, the behavior is identified and a reason why it is important is provided.

> Dear Class,
>
> I appreciate the way you lined up after recess today. You all came quickly and marched quietly back to the classroom. We were able to get back to the classroom without wasting any time.
>
> Sincerely,
>
> Mrs. Coley

3 It is very important to emphasize that only cards about happy happenings are put in the box and that students must sign their contributions to the Happy Happenings Box. A comment can be made about an individual's good behavior or group behavior:

Adam is helping the PE teacher get the equipment ready for PE class. It is important to help others when we can.

—David Cunningham

4 While students should be encouraged to write about their positive observations and put them in the Happy Happenings Box, it is also important to encourage students every day to look for all the good things in others. Some teachers find that this technique works best when a specific block of time is set aside each week for the class members to contribute to the Happy Happenings Box.

5 One day of the week is designated for the teacher to read the comments aloud to the class. The day before reading the comments aloud to the class, the teacher may want to quickly read all the contributions beforehand, just in case a student has written something that is unclear because of handwriting or spelling. The teacher should use this as a "teachable moment" and ask the student to help her figure out what he or she intended to communicate. Another reason for prereading the content of the box is to identify anything that might be inappropriate. Any such cards should simply be discarded.

6 Rather than read the cards aloud at one time, identify several times across the school day when four or five cards can be read aloud—first thing in the morning, before recess, before lunch, after lunch, and at the end of the day.

7 Students love to hear their comments read aloud and the students who have written the comments also love to hear their contribution read aloud by the teacher.

Extension

This activity not only provides students with examples and models of good behavior, kindness, and consideration, it also provides them with a real reason for writing. To add some spice and variety to this activity, the teacher can invite other faculty members, the principal, guests who visit the classroom, or the lunchroom staff to observe the class and contribute something to the Happy Happenings Box.

10

Lifeline
Past–Present–Future

S tudents who do well academically and in life have a vision of what they want to be. They have aspirations for the future. Researchers have found that students who do not do well in school don't see themselves "in the future." The Lifeline: Past–Present–Future activity helps students to see the relationship between their past and present interests and how they might play out in the future.

Focus on Motivation and Literacy Learning

This activity motivates students to have aspirations for the future—a future that builds upon the past and the present. This activity is developed in three stages—past, present, and future—and several days are needed for each stage. As students construct a lifeline of their past, present, and future, they engage in discussions with peers as well as reading and writing activities.

How It Works

1 This activity works best when the teacher models each step: past, present, and future. Begin with the idea of constructing a poster of your past. Reflect on your early memories, for example, a home you lived in, family members, books you had as a child, or a pet. On your poster you might use a few photos, some drawings or illustrations, or words cut from magazines or newspapers. You don't have to do fancy artwork; you can look through magazines to find pictures that remind you

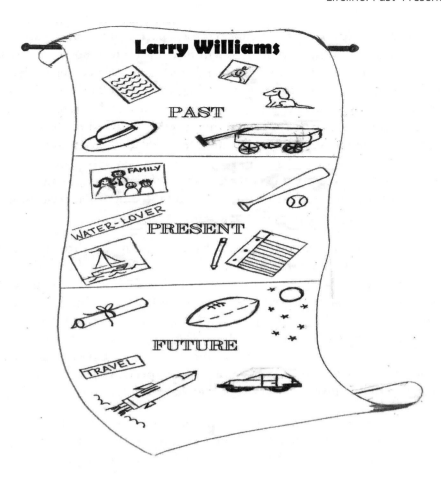

of things in your past. It is very important not to overrely on photographs. Many students in your classroom may have limited photos of their past.

2 The second stage of this activity is to share your past poster with your students—talking about the importance of these things in your past and how these things bring you happy memories. For example, you might have something as simple as a green leaf on your poster to represent love of nature or walking in the woods. Encourage students to think about things in their past that have brought them joy.

3 Tell students that everyone will be constructing a lifeline of things from their past that have brought them joy or pleasure. They can use "real" things that can be pasted on the poster, pictures and words from magazines, photographs, or they can do their own drawing or illustrations. Give students a large piece of construction paper and have them write PAST at the top in large letters (refer to your own poster so they have a model) and write their names on the back of the poster. Give students several days to construct their posters. Provide the students with lots of magazines and newspapers and encourage them to find pictures that represent things in their past that brought them joy.

4 After students have completed their past poster, put the students in groups of four or five. Tell them that they will now have an opportunity to share their past poster with other students. Have students bring their poster to the small group. Set a timer for a minute or two (according to the age/grade of the students) and tell them they will now have an opportunity to share their posters in their small groups. (Remind them that you modeled this when you talked to the class about your past poster.) One student talks for a minute about the past poster and when the timer goes off, the next student talks about his or her past poster, continuing until all students have had a chance to talk about their posters. This stage of the activity provides students with an **opportunity to talk about their past** using concrete representations they have put on their poster.

5 The next day students should have an opportunity to write about their "past." The teacher should model this task by writing about the artifacts on their model poster. Focus on things that are appropriate such as your college degree, favorite books, family, and nature. Then tell the students that they will now have an opportunity to write about their past. This stage of the activity may take a day or two, depending on the age/grade of the students. This stage of the activity provides students with **an opportunity to write about ideas they have represented on their poster** and have talked about with a small group of peers. It is very important that students have an **opportunity to read** what they have written to their small group.

6 When students have completed the writing activity, they can paste their paper on the back of their poster. Be sure to have students write on only one side of the paper so the papers can be pasted to the back of the past poster.

7 The Lifeline past posters can be displayed on the walls of the classroom or in the school hallways.

8 Students now repeat the process with a poster that focuses on the present. When they have constructed a present poster, shared it with their small group and written about their present, the present poster is taped to the bottom of their past poster. At this point, the teacher should emphasize that each student is constructing his or her own Lifeline of their past, present, and future.

9 The process is repeated for the future poster. Again, you should model the process of reflecting on your past and present and how they might influence your future. For example, many teachers take courses toward degrees—if so, you might have a brochure from your college or university with the word "Graduation!" that you could paste on your poster. If you like to travel, you might have magazine pictures of places you might like to see.

10 Students then tape their future posters to the bottom of the present poster . . . and their Lifelines are complete.

Extension

The construction of the Lifeline provides students with an opportunity to construct a representation of things that have brought them pleasure in their past and in the present, and most importantly, it gives them an opportunity to think in positive ways about their future. Lifeline also provides students with an opportunity to *talk* about ideas they have represented on their posters, *write* about the ideas represented on their posters, and *read* what they have written to their small-group members.

PART TWO

Promoting Self-Concept as a Reader

Pause for a moment and consider the following: Is there anything that you think you're just plain "not good at"? If so, what? For example, you may think you're "not a math person" or "not a good runner." If you perceive yourself as "not a good _____" (fill in the blank), do you tend to choose to participate in this activity? Do you think it's possible for you to become a good _____?

We have ample evidence to suggest that when we perceive ourselves as innately weak and incapable of improvement in a particular area, our desire to participate in the activity tends to be low. Few people are motivated to engage in activities that they perceive are their inherent weakness. And why try to improve when we *expect* to fail? Self-concept is at the heart of the "expectancy" component of Eccles's (1983) expectancy–value theory, which proposes that people will choose (or not choose) to participate in activities depending on how well they *expect* to do.

"Self-concept as a reader" refers to the degree to which people perceive themselves competent as a reader. What's particularly interesting—and concerning—is that our self perceptions can become a self-fulfilling prophecy. Students who think of themselves as "good readers" tend to choose to read (they have high motivation), and the sheer act of reading improves their reading performance. On the other hand, students with low self-concept as readers tend not to choose to read (they have low motivation), which minimizes their reading practice, which limits their reading growth. Self-fulfilling prophecy fulfilled!

How can we promote high self-concept as a reader? We might think that telling our students "You're a great reader!" will do the trick, but that message frequently falls on deaf ears. Why? Imagine if your classroom experiences made you believe that you were *horrible at math* (perhaps, for some of you, this isn't hard to imagine)—and your teacher said to you, "You're good at math!". How would you respond? Would you . . . *believe* him or her? Would your personal experience override the positive comment? Chances are the comment will not impact your low self-concept. So, what can be done?

One approach is to identify and share with individual students what they *can do* in specific, descriptive ways so that positive comments are not only true, but they are perceived by the student as honest and true. This technique can also help maintain self-concept for students who perceive themselves as competent readers. In Part Two, *Specific Praise* provides alternatives to general praise (e.g., "Good job!"), which has minimal, if not negligible, impact on self-concept. The technique *I Can, You Can, We Can* involves the teacher in identifying, sharing, and recording specific literacy strengths for the student and also prompting the student to *self-identify* his or her strengths, which is a crucial transition for improving *self-concept*.

As we see with the "horrible at math" example described above, our *experiences* may teach us that we're not "good" at something, and these experiences can profoundly affect our self-concepts. Why might that happen? Frequently it's because the tasks presented to us were not within what Vygotsky (1978) called the "zone of proximal development." The theory of the zone of proximal development suggests that learners benefit from opportunities that offer just the right amount of challenge, that is, opportunities that are not too easy, not too difficult, but "just right" to ensure success *and* growth. *High Five, Now–Next–Quick Reads, Word Sorting for Younger Students* (for grades K–2), and *Word Sorting for Older Students* (for grades 3+) draw upon Vygotsky's notion of the zone of proximal development to boost self-concept and promote literacy learning. Some of these methods maximize motivation by infusing proximal development scaffolding with other powerful motivators, such as choice, interest, and self-regulation.

Lastly, self-concept can suffer profoundly when students perform poorly in front of their peers. Conversely, when students are successful, self-concept is heightened. *Experts Teaching, Every-Pupil-Response Techniques*, and *Alternatives to Cold, Round Robin Reading* are engaging methods that not only hold instructional value, but also help to ensure that all students have an opportunity to shine among their peers.

If you'd like to assess your students' self-concepts as readers, we've included the Motivation to Read Profile (MRP; Gambrell, Palmer, Codling, & Mazzoni, 1996) in the back of this book. The MRP includes two subscales: self-concept as a reader and value of reading. Self-concept scores can be calculated independently from value of reading scores.

Consider This

1 When and how do you praise students? What are some opportunities that you have during the school day to offer specific, descriptive praise? How might simply telling students that they're good readers but that they just need to work harder not be an effective method for boosting self-concept and maximizing motivation?

2 How can identifying a student's literacy strengths help you identify his or her *zone of proximal development* and plan the next steps for instruction? How might you differentiate instruction within your classroom to maximize instructional effectiveness and students' self-concepts as readers?

3 What are some additional ways to provide opportunities for all students to "shine among their peers"?

References

Eccles, J. (1983). Expectancies, values, and academic behaviors. In T. Spence (Ed.), *Achievement and achievement motives: Psychological and sociological approaches* (pp. 75–114). San Francisco: Freeman.

Gambrell, L. B., Palmer, B. M., Codling, R. M., & Mazzoni, S. A. (1996). Assessing motivation to read. *The Reading Teacher, 49*(7), 518–533.

Vygotsky, L. S. (1978). *Mind and society: The development of higher psychological processes.* Cambridge, MA: Harvard University Press.

11

Experts Teaching

This modified Jigsaw (Aronson, Blaney, Stephan, Sikes, & Snapp, 1978) activity received the name "Experts Teaching" from Aaron, an enthusiastic fifth grader, during a unit about North American owls. Aaron explained that his classmates became "experts" during their investigation and were teachers as they planned how to share their new knowledge. Experts Teaching encourages students to take ownership of text as they learn material well enough to teach it to their classmates.

Focus on Motivation and Literacy Learning

Experts Teaching nurtures intrinsic reading motivation by allowing students to choose their group and/or content, learn challenging information, collaborate with peers and the teacher regarding how the information will be taught, and engage in the authentic act of teaching peers. Becoming experts who teach provides students with the opportunity to grow their self-concept as a reader.

How It Works

1 Divide content into chunks that can be studied by groups of students. Depending on grade level, this could involve chunking a chapter, a text, or multiple passages from across a variety of texts. In Aaron's classroom, the chunks were chapters from *The Book of North American Owls* by Helen Sattler. The class read the owl overview (the first chapter) together and then each group was responsible for one chapter in the remainder of the book.

2 Encourage students to browse the text for several days before selecting their group.

3 Allow students to select the group they would like to participate in after the content is chunked. Like *Vote for the Read-Aloud* (Chapter 29), selections can be made using paper ballots with students offering their first and second choice. Holding the group vote after students have browsed the content focuses the vote on the important material to be studied versus who is in the group.

4 After arranging the groups, students become experts by reading and discussing their material.

5 As the groups learn the material, they should engage in several discussions. First, they should talk about their understanding of the material—checking the text to confirm understandings and/or to clarify misunderstandings. In addition, the groups should discuss how they will teach the material to their peers. Teaching options might include, but are not limited to, an oral report, PowerPoint presentation, poster, map, chart, graph, Jeopardy game, poem, interview, play, radio play, game board, and/or I-movie. If the class has access to technology, students can also engage their peers virtually in a blog or wiki space. See below for an example of a guide used by Aaron's teacher to help each group plan its teaching session.

6 After becoming experts in their material and deciding on their presentation mode, students and the teacher negotiate the most important content to be taught to peers and begin moving content from the text to their presentation mode.

Example of an Experts Teaching Planning Guide

Group members: Aaron, David, Michael, William

Text: Chapter 2, "Perfect Predators," from *The Book of North American Owls* by Helen Rooney Sattler

Expert knowledge being presented: predatory style, eyesight, hearing, talons, ears, wings, nocturnal

Method of presentation: PowerPoint and demonstration

Materials needed: Owl pellets and Popsicle sticks

Technology needed: Computer and LCD projector

Time needed: 1 hour

7 Experts Teaching culminates with each group teaching its new knowledge to the class.

8 Celebrate the expertise of the groups by inviting school VIPs to the Experts Teaching presentations.

References

Aronson, E., Blaney, N., Stephan, C., Sikes, J., & Snapp, M. (1978). *The jigsaw classroom.* Beverly Hills, CA: Sage.

Sattler, H. (1998). *The book of North American owls.* New York: Sandpiper.

12

Every-Pupil-Response Techniques

Every-Pupil-Response (E-P-R) techniques let children "show what they know." E-P-R cards allow every child to be purposively engaged in learning. Perhaps the most common form of E-P-R is when teachers ask a classroom of students to respond to a statement by giving "thumbs up" or "thumbs down." Other techniques that allow all students to respond and interact with the teacher include the use of a variety of cards including Yes–No cards, Agree–Disagree cards, 1–2–3 cards, and, for younger children, "smiley face" and "frowny face" cards. Using these simple techniques, every child can be actively engaged in responding to teacher questions and statements. Rather than having one child respond to a question, the teacher can engage all the students (in a group or in the entire classroom) in responding. E-P-R techniques can be used effectively in both small-group and whole-class instruction.

Focus on Motivation and Literacy Learning

When every child has Yes–No cards, the entire class can respond to questions posed by the teacher. Every child is actively involved, and fear of failure is reduced because no student is "put on the spot" to give the correct answer. Research supports the notion that learning is enhanced when students are engaged rather that passive. With E-P-R techniques, every student can demonstrate his or her knowledge to the teacher. And students are free to observe and learn from the responses of their peers in a nonthreatening learning environment. An important tip for using E-P-R techniques is that the teacher focuses on correct or appropriate responses and reinforces learning while ignoring incorrect or inappropriate responses.

E-P-R cards can be used to review a lesson that has been taught, to reinforce learning, and to determine how well children understand what they have read. The use of E-P-R techniques can also provide the teacher with informal and immediate feedback about how a lesson is going. If the teacher notices many incorrect responses, this may indicate that reteaching or review might be necessary.

How It Works

1 The quality of the questions the teacher poses will set the tone for answers that call for a range of responses. To encourage all children to participate, start with some literal-level easy questions, such as "In the story, did Elizabeth move to California? Yes or No?" After all the students have responded, the teacher can then move on to ask follow-up questions that require higher-level thinking by asking individual students "Why do you think so (or why not)?"

2 Teacher modeling is an important component of E-P-R techniques. The teacher should pose questions that can be answered by the particular E-P-R cards being used and should model and reinforce the correct response. For example, with Yes–No cards, the teacher might pose the following question: "Yes or No? A spider has six legs?" The children then respond by showing their Yes or No cards. The teacher holds up the No card, points to a child holding a No card and says, "No, spiders do not have six legs—spiders have eight legs." Note that after the group has responded to the question, the teacher focuses on a child who is showing the correct response and reinforces his or her response. Incorrect or inappropriate responses are ignored.

3 E-P-R techniques are most effective when the teacher creates an environment in which children feel free to change their responses if they are inclined to do so. Often children will notice that the majority of the responses are YES and they have responded with a NO. If a child changes his or her response, it indicates that he or she is engaged and he or she will likely learn and remember the correct information. Research indicates that children learn when they are allowed to correct their own mistakes. E-P-R techniques allow children to observe the responses of their peers if they are uncertain or insecure about their responses. The teacher can quickly note those children who appear to be slow to respond and may be having difficulty in order to provide individual teaching, small-group instruction, or whole-class review.

Other Examples of E-P-R Cards

Picture Cards

For very young children, cards with pictures can be used. Every child would have the same set of E-P-R picture cards at his or her desk, and the teacher would have identical cards for reinforcing and for showing the correct response. Picture cards can be used to answer vocabulary and comprehension questions such as:

- ◆ *Which one can you spend?*
- ◆ *Which card shows a pet?*
- ◆ *Which one might be a dessert?*

Picture cards can also be used to develop proficiency in following directions. The teacher can give directions for children to follow using their cards such as:

- ◆ *Put the dog in the **middle** of your desk.*
- ◆ *Put the balloon **above** the dog.*
- ◆ *Put the ice cream cone **between** the dog and the balloon.*

Concepts such as *over* and *under, above* and *beneath, top* and *bottom, right* and *left, between, beside, opposite,* and the like can be developed using E-P-R cards. In addition, colors and shapes can be taught using picture cards.

1–2–3 Cards

For follow-up activities to read stories or informational text, children can use 1–2–3 cards to respond to questions that require a number response such as:

♦ *How many children were there in the story?*
♦ *How many body parts does an insect have?*
♦ *How many wishes did the fairy grant the old man?*

Word Cards

Cards that have words can be used for responding to questions about stories or informational text. Children have cards with the words *Virginia opossum, kanga-roo,* and *bettong* to answer questions about marsupials, such as the following:

♦ *Which marsupials are nocturnal—they wake up when the sun goes down?* (bettong and Virginia opossum)
♦ *Which marsupial is known for its incredible hopping?* (kangaroo)
♦ *Which marsupial is known for its ability to "play dead"?* (Virginia opossum)

To extend the activity to higher-level questioning, the teacher might ask follow-up questions such as:

♦ *What are the advantages of being nocturnal?*
♦ *How are the Virginia opossum, kangaroo, and bettong alike?*
♦ *How are they different?*

Smiley–Frowny Cards

Cards showing a smiley face and a frowny face can be used to ask children how they felt about a particular story or event in a story. Students can use the cards to respond to questions such as the following:

◆ *How do you feel about this story?*

◆ *Do you think this was a happy or a sad story?*

◆ *How did John feel when he could not go camping?*

With each of these questions, the teacher would want to follow up with individual responses and opinions from children about why they felt this way or what the reasons were that John felt unhappy about not being able to go camping.

Extension

E-P-R techniques can be used as a springboard to higher-level questions after the teacher first involves everyone in responding to a question as in the following exchange: Teacher: "Evan was a brave soldier. Yes or No?" The children then respond with their Yes–No cards. Teacher indicates the child with a correct response: "Yes, he was a very brave solider." If the teacher notices that Sam has responded quickly and enthusiastically, the teacher might take advantage of this observation and call on Sam to respond to probing questions such as "What did Evan do that makes you consider him to be courageous?" Children are thus given an opportunity to first respond individually to a teacher-posed question and after the correct response is reinforced, many children may be encouraged to provide justification and elaboration on their thinking.

Children like using E-P-R techniques because it is a nonthreatening way of responding to teacher questions. Shy children who are reticent about verbally responding frequently "open up" after they have responded correctly with an E-P-R card. After receiving positive reinforcement for a correct response, shy children are often eager to share their reasons for giving a correct answer. Every child can show what he or she knows with E-P-R cards.

When interest and enthusiasm appear to wane in a discussion, E-P-R techniques may be just the thing to get students engaged. E-P-R techniques encourage good listening and good thinking.

13

High Five

igh Five is an easy method that students can use to determine if a book is "just right" for independent reading. Students begin with fingers closed (making a "fist") and read a page from a self-selected book. Each time the student comes to a word he or she doesn't know, he or she extends a finger. If five fingers are extended when the student finishes reading a page, the book is probably too high, or difficult, for them to read without assistance.

Focus on Motivation and Literacy Learning

Self-concept as a reader is enhanced when students read texts they are able to decode and comprehend without assistance. If texts are too difficult, students tend to think of themselves as poor readers. High Five provides students with a sense of self-regulation and independence in self-selecting books that will afford them successful reading experiences. High Five can improve literacy learning by giving students an easy method for self-selecting texts that enable them to read for meaning and to practice known skills and strategies without assistance from others.

     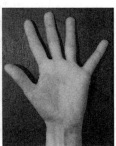

How It Works

Teach students the following method. Be sure to model and provide guided practice to promote students' independent use.

1 Choose a book that you'd like to read.

2 Open to the middle of the book. Find a page with many words.

3 Make a fist with one hand. Begin reading the page and raise a finger every time you cannot read a word.

4 If you get to the end of the page and all five fingers are up, the book is probably too high or difficult for you to read on your own. If you'd like, ask your teacher (or family member) to read the book aloud to you or help you read the book. Try another book to read on your own.

5 If a student wants to read a book that is a "High Five," we advise that you allow the child to read the book. Taking a book away from a child because "It's too difficult for you" can negatively affect self-concept as a reader and the value of reading. We suggest maximizing reading motivation by honoring students' choices (see *Honor All Print* [Chapter 22]). Students should be taught to use High Five only as a general guideline to help them figure out if a text is "just right" in terms of difficulty.

Extension

Be sure to tell students that if they want to read a book that is a "High Five," they can ask a teacher or family member for assistance. You might also consider using the book for a read-aloud.

High Five is a method for students to use to determine if a book is "just right" for them. There are other valid and reliable ways for teachers to match readers to texts. Consider using running records or informal reading inventories to acquire students' independent reading level (reading without assistance), instructional level (reading with assistance), and frustration level (too difficult to read even with assistance). A text's level, or "readability," can be determined using computer programs, included in many word-processing programs, or publisher-assigned text level. There are also source books that list children's books by level, for example, Fountas and Pinnell (2009).

Reference

Fountas, I. C., & Pinnell, G. S. (2009). *The Fountas & Pinnell leveled book list, K–8+: 2010–2012 Edition* (print version). Portsmouth, NH: Heinemann.

14

I Can, You Can, We Can

I Can, You Can, We Can invites the student and the teacher to think about and record student's strengths as a reader or a writer, as well as to plan for future learning. This idea is recommended for use during student–teacher conferences.

Focus on Motivation and Literacy Learning

- ◆ **I Can.** It is critically important for students to be able to self-identify what they can do (*I Can* statements), and not just focus on what they can't do, in order to foster high self-concept as a reader.

- ◆ **You Can.** As teachers, we frequently praise students verbally by saying something like, "Good job!", but the praise is not specific (Good job on what?) and quickly passes. When the teacher shares what students can do specifically and in writing (*You Can* statements), students view the praise as truthful—and the praise has a significant, positive impact on self-concept. *You Can* statements benefit literacy learning because teachers can identify students' strengths in order to design instruction that offers just the right amount of challenge.

- ◆ **We Can.** *We Can* statements include what the student can do with the teacher's help, which also focuses the student's attention on what he or she can do. *We Can* statements may also include next steps about what the student and teacher may work on together. Engaging students in the act of planning for instruction fosters active participation in learning and a sense of self-regulation.

I Can, You Can, We Can has the added benefit of providing a written record of student's strengths. We suggest that students and teachers review I Can, You Can, We Can statements over time to celebrate the student's growth as a reader or writer. Doing so can have a powerful positive impact upon students' self-concept as a reader or writer—and a teacher's self-concept as a teacher!

How It Works

1 Meet with the student in a one-on-one conference. Bring two pencils and the template displayed in Figure 14.1.

- **Complete the *I Can* column.** Tell the student that you noticed that he or she has a number of strengths as a reader (or writer). Ask the student to think about some things he or she is able to do or what he or she has learned. For early or reluctant writers, you may wish to record the student's comments. Do not change the student's words.

- If the student is unable to identify any strengths, move to the "You Can" column. As the student's self-concept is boosted and he or she becomes increasingly aware of strengths over time, the student will be able to identify what he or she can do. When the student does, be sure to include "You can identify what you can do!" in the You Can column.

- **Complete the *You Can* column.** Tell the student about some of the things you've noticed that the student can do and record it in this column. We suggest that you think about the student's strengths as a reader or writer (and perhaps record on a sticky note) before the conference.

- **Complete the *We Can* column.** Say "Let's think about some of the things that you can do with my help." Here, you and the student work together to record what the student can do with your assistance, which can include plans for next steps for learning.

Student name: _____ Teacher name: _____		
Date: _____		
I Can	**You Can**	**We Can**

FIGURE 14.1. I Can, You Can, We Can template.

2 Complete more I Can, You Can, We Can templates with the student as he or she grows as a reader and/or writer (e.g., every 2 weeks, once a month, every semester). Be sure to save the copies and review with the student to build self-concept.

Extension

To help students identify their strengths, improve self-concept, and foster literacy learning, be sure your verbal praise during the school day is specific. See *Specific Praise* (Chapter 15).

For our most struggling readers and writers, we sometimes have difficulty identifying their strengths, but they do exist! Here are some possibilities to consider:

- ◆ What are the student's interests? List them and help the student find books on these topics.
- ◆ Does the student have a favorite book? If so, include the title in your comments.
- ◆ Does the student prefer fiction or nonfiction?
- ◆ Did you overhear the student talking about a particular book?
- ◆ Does the student know some of the purposes for reading and writing?
- ◆ Does the student have a positive attitude about learning to read or write? How can you tell?
- ◆ Did the student enjoy a particular book during read-aloud time?
- ◆ What specific skills and strategies does the student know?
- ◆ Did the student participate in any discussions about a book, including a discussion with a friend?
- ◆ Does the student enjoy the library, listening center, or reading/writing on the computer?

Consider sharing I Can, You Can, We Can statements with parents during parent–teacher conferences. It's important for parents to see what their child can do, too!

15

Specific Praise

Specific Praise involves the teacher identifying what in particular the student is doing (or did) well and using that information to provide positive, descriptive feedback, versus general praise like "Good job!" or "Great work!".

Focus on Motivation and Literacy Learning

We frequently think we're building students' self-concept and promoting learning when we praise students with a general statement like "Terrific job!". But research tells us otherwise (Brophy, 1981; Chalk & Bizo, 2004; Henderlong & Lepper, 2002). Students usually perceive general praise as insincere and without merit. Furthermore, general praise has little educational value because the praise does not reinforce any specific, positive behavior. On the other hand, specific or descriptive praise that reflects what the student did well, such as "You did a great job fixing up that word so that it looks right and makes sense in the sentence," is perceived as sincere and has a positive impact on self-concept, effort, persistence, on-task behavior, and learning. Specific Praise can also help students identify their strengths, which can be used with *I Can, You Can, We Can* (see Chapter 14).

How It Works

1 When you are about to praise, think about what in particular the student is doing (or has done) well. Integrate your observation into your praise. Table 15.1 provides some examples of general praise versus preferred Specific Praise.

2 Be sure to use an honest voice when offering Specific Praise. And whenever possible, praise in private to foster mutual respect.

TABLE 15.1. General versus Specific Praise

General	Specific
"Nice job reading!"	"I really like how you paused at commas, read in phrases, and used an expressive voice. Nice job."
"Good answer."	"Nice work bringing information from the text into your answer."
"You write wonderfully, Galen." *or* "You're a good writer, Galen."	"Galen, I like how you've used an interesting tidbit of information in your introductory sentence. It really pulls me in to want to read more."

3 Be cautious about praising students for their intelligence (e.g., "You're really smart!"). Doing so can actually cause children to *avoid* tasks that might demonstrate that they're "not so smart" (Dweck, 2007; Mueller & Dweck, 1998).

4 Be wary of praising tasks that are easy for the student. In doing so, the student may perceive that you are offering praise because you feel sorry for him or her (Meyer, 1992) or that you don't understand him or her (Henderlong & Lepper, 2002).

5 After Specific Praise, enjoy seeing the smile on your student's face *and* how he or she repeats the positive learning that you've reinforced!

References

Brophy, J. E. (1981). Teacher praise: A functional analysis. *Review of Educational Research, 51*(1), 5–32.

Chalk, K., & Bizo, L. A. (2004). Specific praise improves on-task behaviour and numeracy enjoyment: A study of year 4 pupils engaged in the numeracy hour. *Educational Psychology in Practice, 20*(4), 335–352.

Dweck, C. S. (2007). The perils and promises of praise. *Educational Leadership, 65*(2), 34–39.

Henderlong, J., & Lepper, M. R. (2002). The effects of praise on children's intrinsic motivation: A review and synthesis. *Psychological Bulletin, 128*(5), 774–795.

Meyer W.-U. (1992). Paradoxical effects of praise and criticism on perceived ability. *European Review of Social Psychology, 3*, 259–283.

Mueller, C. M., & Dweck, C. S. (1998). Praise for intelligence can undermine children's motivation and performance. *Journal of Personality and Social Psychology, 75*(1), 33–52.

16

Now–Next–Quick Reads

During Self-selected Reading Time (SRT), students often find that they have
selected a book that is either too hard or boring. Teachers often report their
concern that the students who most need experience and practice reading
are the ones who are often off-task during SRT. These students are the "flippers"
and the "wanderers"—instead of reading during SRT, they can be found flipping
through books or wandering around the classroom trying to find a book to read.
Now–Next–Quick Reads is a procedure that increases time-on-text during SRT.

Focus on Motivation and Literacy Learning

Research suggests that the more you read, the better reader you become. There is
also research evidence to support the important role of choice in motivation. When
students have only one book available during SRT, it is likely that younger and
struggling readers may find that they have selected a book that is too difficult and
better readers may find that they have selected a book that is not very interesting.
The Now–Next–Quick Reads technique is designed to increase the likelihood that
students read during SRT.

How It Works

1 Explain to students that good readers always have a book that they are reading—a "now" book—and good readers almost always have a list of books they
can't wait to read—"next" books—and good readers like to have some quick and
easy reads available just in case they have a few "extra" minutes to read. Quick and
easy reads include poetry books, joke books, riddle books, magazines, newspapers,
Guinness World Records—any book that you can pick up and read for a few min-

utes when you have time. There are great informational books that make excellent quick reads.

2 You may want to have sample books to show students. You might even consider showing them your now book, some of your next books, and what you enjoy as quick reads.

3 Tell students that they need to prepare for SRT by selecting a now book, a next book or two, and at least one quick read.

4 For younger children, a shoe box can serve as a Library Box for storing Now–Next–Quick Reads books. See the illustration in Figure 16.1 for an example. (Tip: These Library Boxes can conveniently be stored on the floor under the whiteboard. If SRT is scheduled after a "special class" where students are out of the classroom, the teacher can greet the students as they return and have them pick up their Library Boxes for SRT as the come into the room.)

5 For upper elementary students, large Ziploc plastic bags (some have a handle) make an excellent storage bag for reading selections.

6 When it is time for SRT, the teacher reminds students that their job is to read what they enjoy reading during this time. It is also time to practice becoming a better reader, and they are to make sure that they read every minute. If they come to

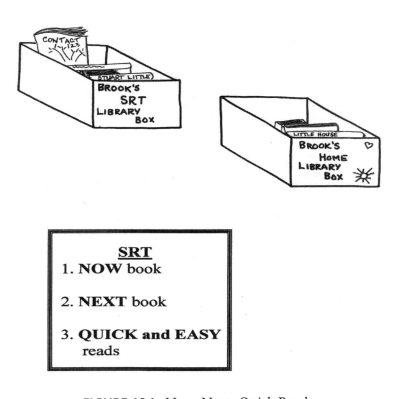

FIGURE 16.1. Now–Next–Quick Reads.

the end of a chapter and want to switch to their quick book, they can do so. If they find they have selected a book they don't like, there will be other books in their box or bag that they can read. This method can substantially increase on-task behavior during SRT. Struggling readers often "save face" by selecting books that are far above their reading level. Observations indicate that these children will often select the "difficult" book and will spend a few minutes doing "pretend" reading. They then move to reading texts that they have selected that are at or near their actual reading level.

Alternatives to Cold, Round Robin Reading

Cold, round robin reading is when students take turns reading aloud without reading the text beforehand (i.e., "cold"). In cold, round robin reading, teachers may choose who will read aloud, students sometimes choose the next person to read (sometimes called "popcorn reading"), or students may volunteer to read aloud. Students need lots of practice reading to improve as readers—but with cold, round robin reading, only a handful of students read portions of text.

Asking students to participate in cold, round robin reading is like asking piano students to play a piece of music that they have not practiced before an audience. Self-concept can suffer with even a single "error" during performance. In fact, during cold, round robin reading, even good readers attempt to read ahead and rehearse their part instead of listening to the student who is reading aloud.

It's a myth that struggling readers improve their word recognition skills by "tracking print" as the fluent reader reads aloud. Quite simply, the struggling reader can't keep up. (Imagine improving your piano skills by "tracking notes" as your piano teacher plays a piece—with perfect fluency!) Cold, round robin reading is not effective practice, even for students who are "good" readers. First, good readers use comprehension strategies such as predicting, self-questioning, summarizing, clarifying, and rereading. Cold, round robin reading does not afford students the opportunity to stop reading and use these comprehension strategies. Second, our strongest readers tend to comprehend better reading silently than aloud.

Focus on Motivation and Literacy Learning

Students rehearsing or silently reading text before reading aloud gives them an opportunity to be successful reading in front of peers, thereby improving self-concept as a reader. Reading aloud for performance creates an authentic purpose for students to read for meaning, to learn and apply decoding skills and strategies, and to practice fluent reading. Rereading texts, which occurs during rehearsal and performance, improves reading fluency. Small-group differentiated instruction using appropriately leveled texts (vs. using one text and cold, round robin reading with more capable students reading aloud for others) can improve students' self-concept as a reader and improve reading achievement because the texts offer just the right amount of challenge.

How It Works

Rehearsing before Reading Aloud

1 If you want students to read aloud, give them an opportunity to rehearse and provide assistance as needed:

- Students may read the text silently and raise their hand or record difficult words on paper, if they need assistance.
- Struggling readers may read the text aloud to you in a one-on-one setting, or a small group of students may "whisper read" the text so that you can prompt decoding and/or comprehension strategies. *Whisper reading* is when students read aloud at their own pace in a "whisper voice" that is loud enough for the teacher to hear, but soft enough not to disrupt their neighbors.

2 Either context is an effective way to assist students prior to reading aloud. Students can then practice reading aloud their particular part with a partner or small group, working on phrasing and reading with expression.

Readers' Theater

Readers' Theater (Rasinski, 2010) involves students reading aloud a story, poem, song, or play. The steps toward performance are described above. However, when reading aloud a story or play, students choose characters and read dialogue. Another student (or students) reads aloud narration. No costumes, props, or stage are necessary, though they may be included for more involved productions. Some tips for Readers' Theater include:

- Begin with easy-to-read texts to instill a sense of success and positive self-concept as a reader.
- Choose texts with many parts so that many students have an opportunity to perform.
- Small groups can choose different texts and perform for the class so that everyone has an opportunity to participate.

◆ Highlight particular parts of the text to help students identify when they are to read.

◆ Make sure all students are fluent and comfortable reading aloud their part before performance.

◆ Perform the text more than once.

◆ Encourage applause at the end of performance to maximize self-concept!

Special Situations

If a particular text is too difficult to decode for some students in your class (even with your assistance) and you are required to use the text for instruction, here are some alternatives to cold, round robin reading:

◆ Perform a teacher read-aloud or a shared read-aloud. A shared read-aloud involves the teacher reading aloud the text and stopping to discuss the text along the way (before, during, and/or after reading). Note that there is no advantage to students following along in their own copy of the text. Doing so can diminish listening comprehension.

◆ Record the text on CD or tape. Less accomplished readers can listen to the text on headphones, while more skilled readers can read the text silently.

If you are not required to use the text for instruction, provide small-group differentiated instruction using leveled texts. For content instruction, you can use leveled texts on the same topic or theme. For example, for a unit on animal habitats, one group could read an appropriately leveled text on desert habitats, another on rain forest habitats, and so on. Students can then share what they learned about their habitat with the class. (See also *Experts Teaching* [Chapter 11].) Everyone then has a chance to demonstrate his or her knowledge to others, thereby enhancing self-concept as a reader.

Cold "buddy reading," where students work in pairs and read parts of the text to each other, is recommended over cold, round robin reading in small groups or the whole class. When students read parts of text to each other in pairs, this can reduce performance anxiety. However, by third grade, we advocate that all students read text silently before buddy reading or engaging in any form of student read-aloud. By this grade level, we need to promote silent reading comprehension.

Reference

Rasinski, T. V. (2010). *The fluent reader: Oral and silent reading strategies for building word recognition, fluency, and comprehension* (2nd ed.). New York: Scholastic.

Word Sorting
for Younger Students

GRADE LEVELS: K–2

Word Sorting for Younger Students is a manipulative activity in which students sort words on individual cards based on phonics, meaning (semantic), or grammatical (syntactic) similarities (Marinak, Mazzoni, & Gambrell, 2012; Zutell, 1998). For grades K–2, we suggest that teachers provide students with words on cards for sorting. Word Sorting may be closed (the teacher tells the students the sorting attribute) or open (students sort words any way that makes sense to them). Optimally, Word Sorting for Younger Students takes place during small-group instruction to minimize the teacher-to-student ratio and maximize personalized, differentiated instruction.

Focus on Motivation and Literacy Learning

The hands-on, manipulative nature of word sorting and students' active participation comparing and contrasting words lends itself to student engagement. To foster students' self-competence as a reader and to promote deep learning through repeated exposure in new contexts, we recommend selecting words for sorting from students' reading, spelling, and/or content-area instruction. This also helps ensure that words for sorting are within students' zones of proximal development. Sorting with a peer provides opportunities for collaborative learning and language use. Open sorts promote student choice and self-direction.

Word Sorting for Younger Students can be used to develop phonics and spelling skills, improve sight word vocabulary, apply knowledge of parts of speech, and increase depth and breadth of vocabulary knowledge.

How It Works

1 Select approximately 10–20 words that target instruction of specific phonics, grammar, or vocabulary skills. Include words from students' reading, spelling, and/ or content-area instruction. Teachers may write words on individual cards for students; however, doing so may be too time-consuming. Alternatively, write or type words for sorting on standard- or legal-sized paper and photocopy. Cut words into "cards" so that each student (or pair of students) has his or her own set for sorting.

2 Ask students to display their words on the desk, unsorted. Ask students to read them in a whisper voice and at their own pace. (Do not use round robin reading; see *Alternatives to Cold, Round Robin Reading* [Chapter 17].) If students do not know a word, say it aloud for them and ask them to repeat it.

Closed Word Sorting

1 Display word cards to head columns. We suggest heading columns with words that are highly familiar. In the example provided in Figure 18.1, *big* and *bike* serve as column headings. Model by thinking aloud, "This word is *big*. The letter *i* in *big* has a short *i*, /ĭ/ sound. This word is *bike*. The letter *i* in *bike* has a long *i*, /ī/ sound."

2 Pick a card, for example, *lip*. Continue thinking aloud, "This word is *lip*. The letter *i* in *lip* has a short *i*, /ĭ/ sound like *big*. I'll put *lip* under *big* because both words have the short *i*, /ĭ/ sound." Note that sorted words should always be placed in columns, not piles, so that students can see all the words they've sorted during the sorting process.

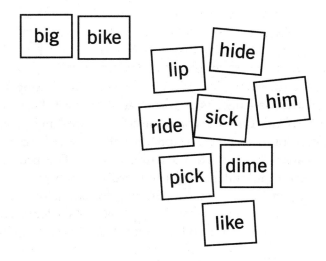

FIGURE 18.1. Closed word sort (example).

3 Continue thinking aloud and modeling the sort using another word card or two, as needed. Note that while there is value in teacher modeling and sorting a few words together as a group, students should always have the opportunity to sort themselves. Motivation and learning are maximized when students actively engage in word sorting using their own set of words and at their own pace. As students become proficient at sorting, you may not need to model for them.

4 Ask students to sort their own set of words using the same column headings.

5 If a student (or student pair) sort a word incorrectly, do not interrupt. To promote self-checking and self-regulation, wait until the student finishes sorting and proceed.

6 When a student (or student pair) finishes sorting, ask the student to read aloud to you the words in each column, saying the sound that is the same in each column. If a student does not identify a word that he or she sorted incorrectly, say, "One of the words in this column needs fixing up. See if you can find it and fix it up."

Open Word Sorting

1 Ask students to sort the words in any way that makes sense to them. Not all words need to be used in sorting.

2 Have students share their sorted words and rationale for sorting. Alternatively, students may display their sorted words, and other students guess their rationale for sorting.

Open word sorts are most successful after students have participated in a number of closed word sorts. Closed word sorts provide students with ideas for open word sorts.

Extension

See Table 18.1 for some ideas for Word Sorting for Younger Students.

To increase challenge, ask students to sort words based on a particular attribute but without giving students words for column headings. To decrease challenge, perform single-column sorts. ("Put together all the words that . . .").

Early readers benefit from Picture Sorting. The process is the same as Word Sorting, except that students say the word for each picture. See Figure 18.2 for an example of a picture sort. Picture Sorting for sounds teaches phonemic awareness. Note that the goal of Picture Sorting is not for students to guess the word for the picture. If students do not know the word for a picture, give them the word.

TABLE 18.1. Ideas for Word Sorting for Younger Students

Phonics	Meaning	Grammar
Number of letters	Antonyms/synonyms	Nouns
Letter recognition (e.g., words that use the letter *p*)	Words that describe specific objects	Verbs
Sounds (beginning, medial, ending) (e.g., words that begin with the /ch/ sound)	Words that are related to specific things or concepts	Adjectives
Word families	Compound words	Singular/plural
Vowels	Contractions	Prefixes, suffixes, root words
Spelling patterns (e.g., CV/CVC/CVCe)		

FIGURE 18.2. Picture sort (example).

References

Marinak, B. A., Mazzoni, S. A., & Gambrell, L. B. (2012). *Reaching all readers strategic reading intervention: Levels AA-S.* Columbus, OH: Zaner-Bloser.

Zutell, J. (1998). Word sorting: A developmental approach to word study for delayed readers. *Reading and Writing Quarterly, 14*(2), 219–239.

19

Word Sorting for Older Students

GRADE LEVELS 3+

Word Sorting for Older Students is a manipulative activity where students sort words on sticky notes in file folders based on phonics, meaning (semantic), or grammatical (syntactic) similarities (Marinak, Mazzoni, & Gambrell, 2012; Zutell, 1998). For grades 3+, we suggest that students copy words for sorting on their own set of sticky notes. Word Sorting for Older Students includes both closed sorts (the teacher tells the students the sorting attribute) and open sorts (students sort words any way that makes sense to them). For older students with little experience at word sorting, sorts may initially take place during small-group instruction so that the teacher can provide immediate and personalized feedback. With increased proficiency, older students sort by themselves or in pairs during independent work time.

Focus on Motivation and Literacy Learning

Word Sorting for Older Students promotes self-competence as students work without teacher guidance. Each student has his or her own file folder and set of words for sorting on sticky notes, which serve as engaging hands-on materials that foster student ownership. To enhance students' self-competence as readers and to promote deep learning through repeated exposure in new contexts, we recommend selecting words for sorting from students' reading, spelling, and/or content-area instruction. This also helps ensure that words for sorting are within students' zones of proximal development. Sorting with a peer provides opportunities for collaborative learning and language use. Open sorts promote student choice and self-direction.

Word Sorting for Older Students can be used to develop word study skills, reinforce understandings of parts of speech, and improve vocabulary knowledge. For these grade levels, we recommend that students sort the same words but in different ways across a 5-day period in order to develop depth and breadth of word learning.

How It Works

If students are not familiar with word sorting, model and provide guided practice using the steps from *Word Sorting for Younger Students*.

1 Select approximately 10 to 15 words from students' reading, spelling, and/or content-area instruction. Write words on the board or on chart paper.

2 Distribute a file folder and 10 to 15 sticky notes to each student (one sticky note per word). Students copy words from the board or chart paper onto sticky notes and may do this during independent work time. Tell students to place all their words onto one side of the file folder, as seen in Figure 19.1.

3 Conduct a closed sort by asking students to sort words by a particular attribute (e.g., words with four syllables). Students then place all the words with four syllables onto the opposite side of the file folder. If students sort during independent work time, they may record their four-syllable words on a recording sheet as displayed in Figure 19.2. In the last row, students write the attribute for the day's sort.

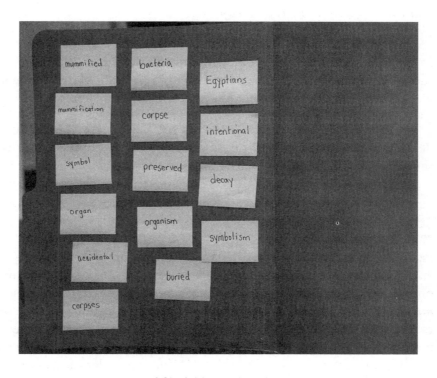

FIGURE 19.1. Use of file folder and sticky notes to sort words.

Day 1	Day 2	Day 3	Day 4	Day 5
symbolism				
intentional				
accidental				
organism				
bacteria				
4 syllable words				

attribute for sorting

FIGURE 19.2. Student word sorting form for recording sorts.

4 Provide students with different attributes for sorting for Days 2 through 4, for example, *words that share the same root word* or *words that share some meaning relationship with the word 'decay.'*

5 On Day 5, conduct an open sort (students sort words any way that makes sense to them) to promote student choice and self-direction. Open word sorts are most successful once students have participated in a number of closed word sorts. Closed word sorts provide students with ideas for open word sorts.

6 Students then share sorted words in small groups. For the Day 5 open sort, students can guess each others' rationales for sorting. Teachers may collect recording sheets for formative or summative assessment.

Extension

Perform some closed word sorts that result in multiple responses by students. For example, if students are asked to sort words that share some meaning relationship, one student may sort *decay, corpse, bacteria*, while another may sort *Egyptians, mummification, symbols*. Ask students for their rationales for sorting. Students' rationales shed valuable insight into their thinking and can serve as excellent formative assessment. Furthermore, multiple responses are effective springboards for small-group discussions. See Table 19.1 for some ideas for word sorting for older students.

TABLE 19.1. Ideas for Word Sorting for Older Students

Phonics	Meaning	Grammar
Vowel sounds (e.g., words that use the long *a* sound, such as *baseball, agent, plain*)	Synonyms/antonyms	Parts of speech
Spelling patterns (e.g., CVV, CVVC, VCCV)	Words with multiple meanings	Past/present tense
Words that share the same sound(s) (e.g., *brow, doubtful, cowardly*; *information, comprehension*)	Homophones (e.g., *ant, aunt*; *sail, sale*)	Singular/plural
Number of syllables	Words that share a meaning relationship	Possessives
Open/closed syllables	Words that describe specific objects	Prefixes, suffixes, root words
Location of accent (first, second, third syllable, etc.)	Compound words	

References

Marinak, B. A., Mazzoni, S. A., & Gambrell, L. B. (2012). *Reaching all readers: Strategic reading intervention: Levels AA–S.* Columbus, OH: Zaner-Bloser.

Zutell, J. (1998). Word sorting: A developmental approach to word study for delayed readers. *Reading and Writing Quarterly, 14*(2), 219–239.

PART THREE

Promoting the Value of Reading

Do you choose to participate in activities that you think are important, interesting, or pleasurable? In other words, do you tend to engage in activities that are *valuable* to you in some way? We imagine you'll answer "Of course!". Now, consider: Have you ever had to study something that you thought lacked value—that was uninteresting or unimportant, sometimes known as . . . boring? If so (and we expect your answer is probably yes), how motivated were you to learn? Did you practically have to force yourself to study? Was your learning superficial, that is, did you do just enough to get by?

The degree to which we *value* a task plays a significant role in whether we choose to participate and fully engage in the task. This is the *value* component of Eccles's (1983) "expectancy–value" theory. Notice that even when an individual *expects* to do well (i.e., has a high self-concept), if the person finds little *value* in the activity, motivation can falter. We expect you've seen students like this in your classroom, who seem to have high self-concepts as readers but are not particularly motivated to read. It may be the case that these children do not *value* reading. Why might this happen and what can be done about it?

First, we need to recognize that some children have limited experience observing or interacting with others who love to read, choose to read, or who read different kinds of texts for different purposes. This sends a tacit message that reading is a "school" activity that no one in "real life" would choose to do or find valuable. And simply telling students "Reading is valuable and here's why . . ." isn't enough. Instead, children need peer and adult role models who don't just "talk the talk" but demonstrate "walking the walk." In Part Three, *Be a Reading Role Model* and *Wall of Fame* describe engaging ways that teachers and students can make their reading public so that experiences, interests, and enthusiasm are communicated with authenticity. Parents and family members also play a crucial role in shaping children's value of reading. In *Promoting the Value of Literacy at Home*, we've included ideas that you can share with parents during conferences or by classroom letter.

We also need to recognize that children—like adults—prefer different kinds of texts and genres. Some adults love comic books and graphic novels. Others are practically addicted to reading cookbooks. Some consume news on the Internet every day or read blogs. Others hate mysteries but can't get enough science fiction. The variations are endless. If we want to boost students' value of reading, we must appreciate their interests and preferences. In *Honor All Print*, we've included an Honor All Print Chart that you can use to record the types of texts your students value, from traditional forms to new literacies. Keep in mind that if we *Honor All Print*, this also means that we need to provide a rich array of reading materials in our classrooms that appeal to a wide variety of interests. Children need opportunities to not only read what they value, but also to try something new. (Try it—you might like it!)

Once you have an idea about the type of texts students enjoy and the topics they find interesting or personally relevant, consider finding some texts that you think particular children might appreciate and extend a *Personal Invitation to Read*. By doing so, you're making meaningful connections between "school reading" and students' personal preferences and lives—an effective method for boosting the value of reading. *Your Life in Books* makes a personal connection by encouraging children to associate books with important events and people in their lives. And *Make a Real-World Connection* uses concrete experiences as a springboard for authentic literacy tasks so that students see real-world value in reading and writing. *Vote for the Read-Aloud, I-Search*, and *Textbook Top 10* use choice, ownership, and exploration to instill task and text value.

We would be remiss not to include some ideas for *Rewarding Reading*. The use of rewards to motivate students to read is an extremely common practice. Quite often, we'll reward students' reading with something students value—like pizza. In *Rewarding Reading*, we offer ideas for rewards that foster reading value—or "rewarding" reading.

If you'd like to assess your students' value of reading, we've included the Motivation to Read Profile (MRP; Gambrell, Palmer, Codling, & Mazzoni, 1996) in Part Five of this book (Forms A, B, and C). The MRP includes two subscales: self-concept as a reader and value of reading. Value of reading scores can be calculated independently from self-concept as a reader.

Consider This

1 Literacy role models that not only "talk the talk" but "walk the walk" are critical for conveying to students the value of reading. How might you share with your students that you read and write—and what you read and write—outside of school? How might you engage other members of your school community in this practice?

2 Imagine the following scenario: A reluctant reader brings a comic book to class to read during sustained silent reading time. Would you say anything to the student about the book? Why or why not? If so, what would you say? Why?

3 Do you reward reading? Why or why not? If so, what types of rewards do you use and under what circumstances? What are some ways to make reading rewarding?

References

Eccles, J. (1983). Expectancies, values, and academic behaviors. In T. Spence (Ed.), *Achievement and achievement motives: Psychological and sociological approaches* (pp. 75–114). San Francisco: Freeman.

Gambrell, L., Palmer, B., Codling, R., & Mazzoni, S. (1996). Assessing motivation to read. *The Reading Teacher, 49*(7), 518–533.

20

Be a Reading Role Model

Teachers are powerful mentors and motivators for their students. When teachers share their reading experiences with students, they communicate the value of reading. The door poster illustrated below is a good way to engage students in talking about what you are reading as well as what they are reading.

Focus on Motivation and Literacy Learning

Many students do not have strong literacy role models in their lives. It is important that students see individuals who enjoy reading for pleasure and for information. Research by the National Assessment of Educational Progress (U.S. Department of Education, 2010) supports the notion that students have higher motivation and reading achievement when their teachers are avid readers who share their enthusiasm for reading.

How It Works

1 Laminate a poster, like the one in the photograph in Figure 20.1, and post it on your classroom door.

2 As you begin reading new books, let students know about it by sharing it on the door poster.

3 Share sections of the book with your students, for example, passages that have a rich description of a character, a sentence with an interesting or descriptive word, or some new bit of information that you learned. As you share your interest and excitement about reading, it will be contagious! As you share parts of books that you are

FIGURE 20.1. Be a Reading Role Model poster (example).

reading, talk with your students about how reading brings you pleasure (e.g., getting lost in a book) and new information (even in fiction we can learn many things about our world). Also, share with your students that reading helps you become a better writer (examples of how authors write a really gripping first paragraph that makes you want to read more) or a better speaker (examples of authors using interesting vocabulary).

4 You can use the door poster to share your personal reading, if you are reading a book that is appropriate for sharing with students (like Miss Davis in Figure 20.1). You can also use the door poster to share children's literature that you are reading.

5 Make this a game-like activity by asking students "What are you reading . . . ?"

Reference

U.S. Department of Education. (2010). *The nation's report card*. Retrieved from *http:// nationsreportcard.gov/reading_2009*.

21

Wall of Fame

Wall of Fame is a method that encourages students to share their passions and celebrate the interests of others. The Wall of Fame is where students and the teacher can publish the print they love best.

Focus on Motivation and Literacy Learning

The Wall of Fame nurtures the value of reading by inviting children to make their reading passions public. Children want to read and are curious about books with which they are somewhat familiar. Familiarity contributes to reading motivation. When children talk about books they most enjoyed reading, they frequently mention that they got interested in a book because they heard about it from a friend, read other books about the character, knew the author, or had read other books in the series. The Wall of Fame is a dedicated place in the classroom for this important sharing.

How It Works

1 Arrange and maintain a "Wall of Fame." This bulletin board is an ever-changing display of reading passions including student favorites (books, magazines, series, etc.), teacher favorites, family favorites, and the principal's choices.

2 Invite your students to publish their favorite titles on the Wall of Fame. Students can publish a single title or maintain a running list of their ongoing and ever-changing favorites. Remember to *Honor All Print* (see Chapter 22), reminding students that the Wall of Fame should reflect the wide variety of print they have enjoyed reading: fiction, nonfiction, poetry, newspaper articles, magazine articles, and web-sites.

3 Encourage students to go to the Wall of Fame when they are looking for a new read!

4 The Wall of Fame can also include the publication of teacher read-aloud titles. If teacher read-alouds are published on the Wall of Fame, it is fun to periodically vote for class favorites.

22

Honor All Print

Honor All Print promotes access to a wide variety of print both for instruction and self-selection. This method defines "print" generously. It affords teachers the opportunity to model and celebrate all forms of traditional and emerging technologies. As Masterman (1985) notes, outside of school, the most influential and widely disseminated modes of communication are visual, oral, and/or aural. Even traditional print is coming to be regarded as a visual medium. Layout, design, and typography are widely understood to be a significant part of the total communicating process. It is important for students at all grade levels to read and respond to a wide variety of traditional print and new literacies.

Focus on Motivation and Literacy Learning

Honor All Print nurtures an appreciation for the value of reading by celebrating the wide variety of interests present in any classroom. In addition to acknowledging interest, Honor All Print promotes the concept that a rich reading life is comprised of all types of text: fiction, nonfiction, newspapers, magazines, Web-based material, and so on. And finally, Honor All Print provides teachers with the opportunity to model reading and responding to a variety of print for a variety of purposes.

How It Works

1 Begin by surveying the reading interests of your students using the Honor All Print Survey (Form G at the end of Part Five of this book). However, view the survey results as a discussion starter. Reading and text interest change over time.

2 Hold small-group conferences to discuss the survey responses. Encourage children to elaborate on their responses. Having children discuss the survey in small groups might prompt children to share additional interests.

3 During read-aloud or *Book Blessing* (see Chapter 1), share a variety of print about topics of interest in your class. In addition to sharing the text, use the opportunity to briefly discuss the type of print being "honored." Explain the type of print, the purpose for reading it, and how it might be read. See Figures 22.1 and 22.2 for examples. A blank version you can use is found in Form 22.1.

Extension

Honor All Print can be used to model a wide variety of desirable reading practices including credible sources. This method can also be a way to broaden student interest. You could make public an Honor All Print display about a topic students have not identified as an interest. See an example of such a display below. And finally, an Honor All Print bulletin board can be arranged. Such a display celebrates the wide variety of print being read by everyone in the class and can serve to nurture new interests. Be sure to include school VIPs in your celebration, as shown in the example in Figure 22.3. A blank version is found in Form 22.2.

References

Ginsburg, D. (2011). Orioles celebrate 4–3 win over Red Sox. Retrieved from *http://news.yahoo.com*.

Glenn, M. (1999). *Foreign exchange: A mystery in poems.* New York: HarperTeen.

Hatkoff, J., Hatkoff, I., & Hatkoff, C. (2011). *Winter's tail: How one little dolphin learned to swim again.* New York: Scholastic.

Howe, J. (2000). *Dew drop dead.* New York: Atheneum.

Masterman, L. (1985). *Teaching the media.* New York: Routledge.

Monks of New Skete. (2011). *The art of raising a puppy.* New York: Little, Brown.

Osborne, M. (1997). *Dolphin at daybreak.* New York: Random House Books for Young Readers.

Sloan, C. (2005). *How dinosaurs took flight: The fossils, the science, what we think we know, and mysteries yet unsolved.* New York: National Geographic Children's Books.

Time's person of the year. (2011). Retrieved from *www.time.com/time/person-of-the-year*.

Western saddles. (2012). Retrieved from *www.saddleonline.com*.

Students' Interest	Bottlenose dolphin; grades 2–4				
Text Shared	<u>Winter's Tail: How One Little Dolphin Learned to Swim Again</u> by Juliana Hatkoff, Isabella Hatkoff, and Craig Hatkoff	Bottlenose Dolphin; http://animals.nationalgeographic.com/animals/mammals/bottlenose-dolphin/?source=A-to-Z	<u>Dolphins at Daybreak</u> by Mary Pope Osborne	Dolphins save surfer from becoming shark's bait MSNBC 8/11/2007 www.msnbc.msn.com/id/21689083	"Dolphins know each other's names" <u>The London Times</u> 5/7/2006
Type of Text	Nonfiction book	Web article from <u>National Geographic</u>	Fantasy fiction	Web article and video from MSNBC	Newspaper article from <u>The London Times</u>
Purpose	To learn how an injured dolphin received an artificial tail and learned to swim again	To learn where dolphins live and what sound they make	To be entertained by a fantasy fiction	To learn about how dolphins and humans interact with each other	To learn about research being done with dolphins
How Can It Be Read?	Entire book or selected chapters	Chunks— map and audio	Entire book	Entire article Chunks— guided by headings Video	Entire article Chunks— guided by five Ws and the inverted pyramid style of a newspaper article

FIGURE 22.1. Honor All Print Chart (example 1).

Honor All Print

Topic: <u>Mysteries</u>

Possible Texts	<u>Dew Drop Dead</u> by James Howe	<u>How Dinosaurs Took Flight: The Fossils, the Science, What We Think We Know, and Mysteries Yet Unsolved</u> by Christopher Sloan	<u>Foreign Exchange: A Mystery in Poems</u> by Mel Glenn	Mystery from the Deep: The Puzzling Case of the Whalefish; <u>http://ocean. si.edu/ocean-photos/ mystery-deep-puzzling-case-whalefish</u>
Type of Text	Fiction	Nonfiction	Fiction story told in poems	Web article from the Smithsonian
Purpose	To be entertained by a fiction mystery	To learn about real unsolved mysteries	To be entertained by mystery poem	To learn about a marine mystery
How Can It Be Read?	Entire book	Entire book Chunks— guided by chapter titles or headings	Entire book	Entire article Chunks— guided by the clues Chunks— guided by hot links in the article Audio

FIGURE 22.2. Honor All Print Chart (example 2).

Honoring All the Print We Are Reading!

Mrs. Smith's Grade 4 Class

Student	Text	Type of Text	Purpose	How Did I Read It?
Eric	Orioles celebrate 4–3 win over Red Sox by David Ginsburg	Newspaper article	To find out who won the game.	Chunk—box score
Molly	Western saddles	Web article	To learn about a new saddle for my horse.	Chunks—guided by headings
Mrs. Smith	Time's Person of the Year	Magazine article	I wanted to learn who Time picked as its person of the year.	Entire article
Mr. Brown, our principal	The Art of Raising a Puppy by The Monks of New Skete	Nonfiction	I need to learn how to begin training my new golden retriever puppy.	Chunks—guided by chapter titles

FIGURE 22.3. Honor All Print Chart (example 3).

Honor All Print Chart

Students' Interest					
Text Shared					
Type of Text					
Purpose					
How Can It Be Read?					

Honor All Print Chart

Honoring All the Print We Are Reading!

Student	Text	Type of Text	Purpose	How Did I Read It?

23

Personal Invitation to Read

Teacher language and practices can powerfully influence how your students see themselves as readers (Edwards, 2011). Personal Invitation to Read is an opportunity for teachers to demonstrate the importance of reading and, more importantly, to personally connect with students about individual text and topic interests.

Focus on Motivation and Literacy Learning

Personal Invitation to Read allows teachers to nurture the value of reading by personalizing text choices for their students. This method can be a powerful reminder that you know what a student enjoys reading. It can invite students to try new text or topics. Or, perhaps most profoundly, Personal Invitation to Read can invite reluctant or struggling readers into text that you have selected especially for them.

How It Works

1 Observe what your students are reading. Listen to their book discussions. Take note of what they check out of the library. If necessary, survey their reading interests. For a quick survey, see the *Honor All Print Survey* (Form G), which can be found in Part Five. For struggling and/or reluctant readers, consider using the Honor All Print Survey to guide a one-on-one discussion.

2 After learning about your students' text and/or topic interests, establish a Personal Invitation to Read Schedule that invites each student in your class into a text. In your planning, consider individual reasons for initiating a Personal Invitation to Read, the text you would provide, and when and how you might extend the invitation. And be sure to jot down a few notes about results. Notes regarding the results of your Personal Invitations to Read can help plan future book talks, invitations, research projects, and so on. See the example schedule provided in Figure 23.1. A blank version is found in Form 23.1.

3 Begin issuing Personal Invitations to Read to your class! Be creative in how you issue the invitations. Wrap books in fun wrapping, newsprint, comics, or (as in the case of reluctant adolescents) perhaps a brown paper bag. I issue invitations verbally, with notes, or by using a preprinted invitation. Place the text and the invitation in a variety of locations—on the child's desk or in his or her locker, backpack, or lunch box.

Extension

One extension for a Personal Invitation to Read is requesting that the school and/ or community VIP issue carefully selected invitations. Another extension, consistent with the zone of proximal development (Vygotsky, 1978) is to include students in the invitations. Suggest that students issue a Personal Invitation to Read to classmates. Having students issue invitations to each other is a great way to encourage your class to become aware of each other's text and topic interests, share text, encourage evaluation, and promote note writing.

References

Edwards, J. (2012). Which words invite students to learn? Retrieved from *http://ascd.type-pad.com/blog.*

Riordan, R. (2008). *39 Clues: The maze of bones.* New York: Scholastic.

Storer, P. (1997). *Your puppy, your dog: A kid's guide to raising a happy, healthy dog.* New York: Storey.

Vygotsky, L. S. (1978). *Mind in society: The development of higher psychological processes.* Cambridge, MA: Harvard University Press.

Mrs. Martin's Grade 4 Class

Student	Reason	Text	Date	Invitation	Result
Jason	Celebrate his family rescuing a puppy and introduce him to an informational how-to text.	<u>Your Puppy, Your Dog: A Kid's Guide to Raising a Happy, Healthy Dog</u> by Pat Storer	September—after his mother wrote a note explaining the family's new addition.	Gift wrapped in paper with paw print.	Discussed the book with me and said his family also read the book. Completed a 6-month photo documentary chronicling the growth and training of his puppy.
Martha	Support her love of horseback riding competitions and introduce her to a newspaper series.	Newspaper series about a competition she and her horse participated in.	November (during the competition)	Sealed in an envelope with her name in the outline of a ribbon.	Shared her experiences with the class and explained how reading books and articles helped her learn about the sport.
Heather	Encourage a reluctant reader who plays mystery videogames.	<u>39 Clues: The Maze of Bones</u> by Rick Riordan	October	Sealed in a brown paper bag on her desk with a personal note inside.	Passed it back to me in a brown paper bag with a note that she loved the book and a request for another—in a brown paper bag.
Mark	Support his love of college basketball and introduce him to the information in sports programs.	Game-day program from Duke versus North Carolina game	January (during college basketball season)	On desk with a personal note explaining how I obtained the program.	I observed him reading it cover to cover, and he wrote about what he learned in his reading log.

FIGURE 23.1. Personal Invitation to Read Schedule (example).

Personal Invitation to Read Schedule

_____

Student	Reason	Text	Date	Invitation	Result

24

Make a Real-World Connection

M̲ake a Real-World Connection involves students engaging in concrete experiences prior to reading and writing in order to stimulate interest and curiosity about a particular topic.

Focus on Motivation and Literacy Learning

When students make real-world connections to reading and writing, this increases their value of literacy because they perceive reading and writing as relevant and worthwhile. Concrete, real-world experiences before reading nonfiction texts can spark interest, excitement, and curiosity about the topic and improve students' reading comprehension (Anderson, 1998; Guthrie et al., 1998, 2000).

How It Works

1 Provide a relevant, concrete experience before reading a nonfiction book. The following examples vary from more to less concrete:

- ◆ Display a real-world object for students (e.g., rocks, oil, worm, cricket). If possible, students may search for the object at a particular location. Invite students to use relevant senses to investigate the object.

- ◆ Demonstrate a science experiment or, preferably, engage students in a hands-on science activity.

- ◆ Display one or more photographs related to upcoming reading, for example, swamps, hurricanes, habitats, oil spills, an event in history.

- ◆ Invite an adult to talk about his or her experience related to an upcoming topic.

2 Engage students in discussion about the object, experience, or the like. Record notes on chart paper. You can use a K-W-L (Ogle, 1986) chart (see Figure 24.1), recording notes in the "Know" column. We encourage you to record notes on sentence strips so that information may be sorted by category (e.g., category: birth—How are worms born? Do worms lay eggs? How many worms are usually born at one time? How do worms take care of their young?). Sorting by category is an extension of the K-W-L known as K-W-L Plus (Carr & Ogle, 1987). Misconceptions may be recorded under the "Know" column. Encourage students to revisit the list during and/or after reading to identify misconceptions. Make changes, as needed.

3 Invite students to pose questions about the object, experiment, or the like. Again, consider writing questions on sentence strips and guide the students to sort the questions by category.

4 Students search for answers to their questions in texts, then share what they've learned with others. Teams may research particular sets of questions if they are grouped by category. (See also *I-Search* [Chapter 25] and *Experts Teaching* [Chapter 11].)

5 Students share new learning. Information may be recorded on sentence strips and placed under the "What I Learned" column or under categorized questions. Revisit "What I Know" so that students may make changes to any misconceptions.

Topic: _____

What I Know	What I Want to Know	What I Learned

FIGURE 24.1. K-W-L chart.

Extension

- ◆ You may need to model generating and categorizing questions. If so, think aloud for students to make your sorting public.

- ◆ When students read texts to answer their questions, provide a variety of texts at varying levels of difficulty, if possible.

- ◆ Encourage students to record any interesting facts that they learned during reading, even if they are unrelated to their particular questions.

- ◆ While concrete experiences prior to reading can spark interest in a particular topic, they do not need to be limited to "before reading." For example, hands-on science activities can be integrated effectively within reading/writing experiences. Also, it may be appropriate for students to engage in some reading for the purpose of asking meaningful questions of an adult who's been invited to speak about his or her experience related to a topic.

References

Anderson, E. (1998). *Motivational and cognitive influences on conceptual knowledge acquisition: The combination of science observation and interesting texts.* Unpublished doctoral dissertation, University of Maryland, College Park.

Carr, E., & Ogle, D. (1987). K-W-L Plus: A strategy for comprehension and summarization. *Journal of Reading, 30*(7), 626–631.

Guthrie, J. T., Cox, K. E., Knowles, K. T., Buehl, M., Mazzoni, S., & Fasculo, L. (2000) Building toward coherent instruction. In L. Baker, M. J. Dreher, & J. T. Guthrie (Eds.), *Engaging young readers: Promoting achievement and motivation* (pp. 209–237). New York: Guilford Press.

Guthrie, J. T., Van Meter, P., Hancock, G., Alao, S., Anderson, E., & McCann, A. (1998). Does concept-oriented reading instruction increase strategy use and conceptual learning from text? *Journal of Educational Psychology, 90*(2), 261–278.

Ogle, D. M. (1986). K-W-L: A teaching model that develops active reading of expository text. *The Reading Teacher, 39,* 564–570.

25

I-Search

An I-Search (Macrorie, 1988) is a research strategy that invites readers to create their own questions, identify sources, and formulate answers. This method encourages students to take ownership of text by constructing their own investigations.

Focus on Motivation and Literacy Learning

I-Search nurtures intrinsic reading motivation by allowing students to take control of the research process. During an I-Search, students make a series of important decisions. They choose the topic to be investigated, write questions to guide their research, identify the text sources to be used, and then complete the matrix. In other words, the "I" in an I-Search is each student engaged in the authentic act of personal investigation.

1 An I-Search chart can be created for either fiction or nonfiction. See the informational text example in Figure 25.1. A blank version is available in Form 25.1.

2 Students begin by selecting a research topic or question.

3 Students then create their guiding questions.

4 After they write guiding questions, students identify the text sources they will use to answer their guiding questions.

5 Critical reading and thinking is encouraged during an I-Search. By virtue of how the matrix is arranged, students will have the opportunity to research the same question across multiple sources, comparing and contrasting the information.

SOURCES	QUESTIONS				
	What was Negro League baseball?	Why did the Leagues flourish?	Who were some of the stars of the Leagues?	What hardships did the players endure?	Why were Leagues important in the African American community?
Trade Books					
Podcasts/Videos					
Websites					
Reference Books					
Magazines					
Newspapers					
Summary					

FIGURE 25.1. I-Search informational text example: Search for Negro League baseball.

6 After completing the matrix, students use the answers to their questions to write a summary of what they learned.

7 An I-Search can conclude when the research and summary have been completed, or an I-Search can be used as a planning process for more in-depth research and writing.

Reference

Macrorie, K. (1988). *The I-Search paper* (2nd ed.). Portsmouth, NH: Boynton/Cook.

FORM 25.1

I-Search Chart

	QUESTIONS				
SOURCES					
Trade Books					
Podcasts/ Videos					
Websites					
Reference Books					
Magazines					
Newspapers					
Summary					

26

Textbook Top Ten

Everyone stays up late to enjoy David Letterman's *Late Show* Top Ten list. The Textbook Top Ten is a reading-thinking method that invites students to crack the code of their textbooks by using Letterman's popular monologue. To complete the Textbook Top Ten, students explore their content-area textbook for the purpose of identifying the text features that can aid or confound their comprehension.

Focus on Motivation and Literacy Learning

Textbook Top Ten is a method that recognizes what Brophy (1999) calls the "motivational zone of proximal development" (p. 77). Specifically, this method nurtures the value of reading by carefully scaffolding students toward independent reading of their textbooks. Motivation theory suggests that learning the predictable (or not) nature of textbooks can lead to a "scaffolded appreciation" of the information in content tools and resources (Brophy, 1999, p. 82).

How It Works

1 A Textbook Top Ten can be created for any textbook or informational text. Explain that the Textbook Top Ten is the ten feature attributes—ranging from least important to most important—that could help or hinder comprehension of the textbook. For example, if important vocabulary is not identified in the same way across chapters, comprehension could be more challenging.

2 It is helpful for teachers to provide students with questions to focus their search. Some examples are below:

◆ Does the textbook have a table of contents?

◆ Does the textbook have a glossary?

◆ Are there chapters?

◆ Are the titles handled the same way for each chapter?

◆ Are there headings?

◆ Are the headings handled the same way in each chapter?

◆ Are there subheadings?

◆ Are the subheadings handled the same way for each chapter?

◆ Are there aids for the readers such as maps, graphs, charts, diagrams, photographs, illustrations, captions, etc?

◆ Are the aids for the reader labeled in the same way for each chapter?

◆ How is important vocabulary handled in the textbook (e.g., no special denotation, bolded, italicized, highlighted, or a combination)?

3 After reviewing the Textbook Top Ten focus questions, students can work alone or in pairs to begin browsing and identifying their Top Ten attributes.

4 After browsing the textbook, have students complete the Textbook Top Ten. The template requires students to list and prioritize their ten attributes and explain why it is important for them to be aware of each attribute. For an example of a completed Textbook Top Ten, see Figure 26.1.

5 After creating Textbook Top Tens, invite students to share their list, explaining why each attribute was selected and why it is important for them to understand each. Invite students to revise their list if they hear a better idea.

6 Ask students to keep their Textbook Top Ten in a reading or content-area folder and to browse it periodically as they are using the textbook.

References

Brophy, J. (1999). Toward a model of the value aspects of motivation in education: Developing appreciation for particular learning domains and activities. *Educational Psychologist, 34*(2), 75–85.

Winkler, P. (2002). *The human body: Keeping fit.* New York: National Geographic Society.

Attribute	Why is it important for me to know this?
10. Table of Contents	• The TOC can help me locate important information. • The TOC is printed on a photograph in white ink. It is hard to read.
9. Textbook Introduction	• Book begins with a two-page introduction that explains the major ideas of the book. • Reading the introduction can help activate my prior knowledge.
8. Picture This and Thinking Like a Scientist	• Each chapter has an extra section. • Are different in each chapter • Reading the extras can help me clarify important information from the chapter.
7. There are charts, graphs, illustrations, and photographs.	• Reading and studying this information will help me understand the main ideas of each chapter.
6. Charts, graphs, illustrations, and photographs are always labeled in red.	• The red label will help remind me to read and study this information.
5. Each chapter begins with a paragraph containing the main idea of the chapter. This paragraph is always in purple.	• Reading this paragraph will help me begin thinking about the major ideas of the chapter. • The purple color will help remind me to look for them and read these paragraphs.
4. Subheadings are statements and questions. They are always printed in black.	• Reading the subheadings can help me comprehend and remember the supporting details related to the main idea. • I need to be on the lookout for both statements and questions. • Knowing they are always in black will help me to look for them.
3. Chapter headings are always statements. They are always printed in yellow.	• Reading the headings can help me clarify the main idea of the chapter. • Knowing they are always in yellow will help me to look for them.
2. Glossary	• All bolded vocabulary words in the book are defined in the glossary. • I can look up vocabulary definitions in the glossary. • I know I can find definitions for all the bolded words in the glossary.
1. Important vocabulary is always bolded.	• Bolding the vocabulary words helps me find and pay attention to the important words for each chapter.

FIGURE 26.1. Textbook Top Ten (example).

27

Rewarding Reading

After five decades of research, questions still remain about the effect of extrinsic rewards on intrinsic motivation. The debate can be seen recently as educators and economists debate the practice of paying students to take tests or attend school. However, research over the past two decades has consistently suggested that it is not a question of whether rewards enhance or undermine intrinsic motivation (Cameron & Pierce, 1994; Deci, Koestner, & Ryan, 1999), but rather under what conditions rewards undermine intrinsic motivation (Cameron, 2001; Deci, Koestner, & Ryan, 2001). Therefore, perhaps it is helpful to consider the word *reward* as a verb (how do we reward reading) or an adjective (what causes reading to be a rewarding experience) versus a noun (the reward) (Marinak & Gambrell, 2009).

Focus on Motivation and Literacy Learning

Rewarding Reading encourages teachers to nurture the value of reading by carefully considering how to make reading rewarding for students. In some cases, such as reluctant and/or struggling readers, this might involve the limited use of extrinsic, tangible rewards. However, for most students, reading becomes rewarding based on the social interactions about text that are arranged within a community of readers.

How It Works

1 Consider the proximity of the reward to the desired behavior when using extrinsic, tangible rewards (Gambrell, 1996). In other words, if you see the need to offer an extrinsic, tangible reward to reluctant and/or struggling readers, consider rewarding reading with a book (vs. other extrinsic, tangible rewards such as tokens or food).

2 Reward reading with authentic tasks. This might include rewarding reading with more time to read or go to the library. Or invite children to be involved in the authentic reading activities in your classroom and school. This includes having a voice in selecting the books for the classroom and/or school library as well as voting for the teacher read-aloud. (See *Vote for the Read-Aloud* [Chapter 29].)

3 Arrange pen pals (adults or students) to write about shared book experiences. Such exchanges could take place within the school and be a school–community project. And the written exchanges could take place using traditional letters or new literacies such as e-mails and/or blogs.

4 Hold book clubs as a periodic alternative to self-selected reading time. During book clubs, allow students to choose their title from a variety of texts that you have multiple copies of (e.g., books, newspapers, article magazines). Consider the Web as one option for a book club. This group could select current event articles or articles of topical interest from credible websites. Each book club then reads the same title and has the opportunity to talk about the text. Encourage the groups to critically discuss text by using higher order prompts such as Socratic questions. You will find some examples of Socratic questions in Figure 27.1.

References

Cameron, J. (2001). Negative effects of reward on intrinsic motivation—a limited phenomenon: Comment on Deci, Koestner, and Ryan (2001). *Review of Educational Research, 71*(1), 29–42.

Cameron, J., & Pierce, W. D. (1994). Reinforcement, reward, and intrinsic motivation: A meta-analysis. *Review of Educational Research, 64,* 363–423.

Changing Minds. (2012). Socratic questions. Retrieved from *http://changingminds.org/ techniques/questioning/socratic_questions.htm.*

Deci, E. L., Koestner, R., & Ryan, R. M. (1999). The undermining effect is a reality after all—Extrinsic rewards, task interest, and self-determination: Reply to Eisenberger, Pierce, and Cameron (1999) and Lepper, Henderlong, and Gingras (1999). *Psychological Bulletin, 125,* 692–700.

Clarifying the Concept	Probing Assumptions	Probing Evidence or Reasons	Questioning Viewpoints	Probing Implications
Can you give me an example?	How did you choose that assumption?	What evidence do you have for your suggestion?	What is an alternative way of looking at this?	What are the consequences of your assumption?
How does this relate to what we have been talking about?	How can you verify that assumption?	What do you think is the cause of this?	What is the difference between . . . and . . . ?	How does this fit with what we learned before?

FIGURE 27.1. Socratic questions.

Deci, E. L., Koestner, R., & Ryan, R. (2001). Extrinsic rewards and intrinsic motivation in education: Reconsidered once again. *Review of Educational Research, 71*(1), 1–28.

Gambrell, L. (1996). Creating classroom cultures that foster reading motivation. *The Reading Teacher, 50*, 4–25.

Marinak, B., & Gambrell, L. (2009, April 7). Rewarding reading?: Perhaps authenticity is the answer. *Teachers College Record*, pp. 1–6. Retrieved from *www.tcrecord.org/content.asp?contentid=15608*.

28

Your Life in Books

Your Life in Books promotes wide reading by encouraging children to connect books with important events and people in their lives.

Focus on Motivation and Literacy Learning

Your Life in Books nurtures the value of reading by celebrating lifelong listening and reading. Inviting children to share their special books is a reminder of the important role reading plays in their lives. And prominently displaying this special collection celebrates each child's individual accomplishment.

How It Works

1 Explain to children that they will have the opportunity to share their life in books.

2 Model examples of your life in books. Show children several of the important books from your life. Explain when you listened (as a read-aloud) or read each. Discuss what else was happening in your life and how each book connected to important events. For an example, see the box on Mrs. Marinak's Life in Books.

3 Explain to children that going home and talking to family is the first step in making their My Life in Books list. Reminiscing with family and revisiting the family library will help them remember favorite read-alouds and books. Talking with family about books will contextualize the titles (e.g., How old was I? What was happening in our life at the time?).

> ### *Mrs. Marinak's* My Life in Books
>
> ◆ *Mike Mulligan and His Steam Shovel* was one of the first read-alouds I remember my mother sharing with me. I loved it because they were building a house down the street at the time. I could enjoy Mike and his steam shovel and then go watch the real thing in action!
> ◆ *Harriet the Spy* is the first chapter book I remember reading. I loved it. I read and reread it. I began "people watching" and keeping a journal about what I saw.
> ◆ I read *Nicholas and Alexandra* the summer before I began high school. It was a romantic epic that I could not put down. What a great love story! After reading *Nicholas and Alexandra*, I read other books about Russian history. I still reread this book every summer. It is not summer until I read *Nicholas and Alexandra*.

4 After talking with family, children should begin their list. In addition to compiling a list, invite children to connect the book with life by writing down what was happening at the time they heard or read each title. You will find an example of a student's Life in Books in Figure 28.1. A blank version you can use is found in Form 28.1.

5 In addition to reminiscing about their life through books, encourage children to collect copies of the books for sharing with the class.

6 Provide a time for children to share their life in books! Since there are numerous children with potentially several books, arrange a schedule so that each child has a time share and the discussion does not prove disruptive to instruction. For example, set aside 15 minutes once a week for My Life in Books.

References

Brown, M. (2007). *Goodnight moon.* New York: HarperFestival.

Burton, V. (1939). *Mike Mulligan and his steam shovel.* Boston: Houghton Mifflin.

Fitzhugh, L. (2001). *Harriet the spy.* New York: Yearling.

Massie, R. (1967). *Nicholas and Alexandra.* New York: Atheneum.

Rylant, C. (1996). *Henry and Mudge: The first book.* New York: Simon Spotlight.

Seuss, D. (1957). *The cat in the hat.* New York: Random House Books for Young Readers.

Simon, S. (2002). *Fighting fires.* New York: Perfection Learning.

Van Allsburg, C. (2009). *The polar express.* Boston: Houghton Mifflin.

Student name: <u>Dante</u>

Book Title	What Was Happening in My Life?	Did I Find a Copy of the Book to Share?
<u>Goodnight Moon</u>	My mom read this book to me every night when I was little. Then I read it to her.	Yes
<u>The Cat in the Hat</u>	My grandma read this book to me over the phone the night before I started kindergarten.	Yes
<u>The Polar Express</u>	My dad reads this to us every Christmas. It's a tradition. And my kindergarten teacher read it to us and gave each of us a silver bell to wear all day long.	Yes
<u>Henry and Mudge: The First Book</u>	This was the first chapter book I read all by myself in kindergarten.	Yes
<u>Fighting Fires</u>	I bought this book at the National Fallen Firefighters Museum. We visited there when I was in first grade because my dad is a firefighter. He said this book is what it is like to be a firefighter.	Yes

FIGURE 28.1. My Life in Books (example).

My Life in Books Chart

Student name: _____

Book Title	What Was Happening in My Life?	Did I Find a Copy of the Book to Share?

29

Vote for the Read-Aloud

Vote for the Read-Aloud addresses concerns raised in a number of studies that indicate that children do not enjoy teacher read-alouds and/or would like more choice in the books being read aloud.

Focus on Motivation and Literacy Learning

Vote for the Read-Aloud encourages ownership in a critical literacy activity by inviting children to help choose the teacher read-aloud. In addition to voting for the teacher read-aloud, this suggestion also promotes browsing and collaboration about the books and periodicals. Affording choice and arranging opportunities for children to browse the book basket and discuss their upcoming vote can nurture appreciation of the value of literacy.

How It Works

1 Consider inviting children to participate in the selection of the teacher read-aloud by arranging the opportunity for a class vote.

2 Begin by arranging a basket of six to eight possible read-aloud titles. In order to honor all print, make sure the basket includes fiction, nonfiction, and periodicals (magazines, newspaper articles). In addition, try to select new books and periodicals, as well as a variety of text that would address the varied interests in a classroom.

3 After arranging a fun-filled basket of potential read-alouds, explain to the children they will have the opportunity to vote for the next teacher read-aloud.

4 Conduct a *Book Blessing* (see Chapter 1). Briefly book-talk each title in the basket, being careful to pique interest but not reveal too much of the story or content.

5 After book-talking each title, explain to the children that the book basket will be available for several days. Encourage children to "inform" their vote by browsing the titles and talking with each other. Enjoy the book basket negotiation that will most likely occur (e.g., "If you vote for my favorite this time, I'll vote for yours next time!").

6 After several days of book basket browsing, invite children to vote for the read-aloud. To maintain control while voting, explain to children that voting will be done on paper (vs. by show of hands). Ask children to vote for their number-one and number-two selections. Explain that though they might not get their first choice this time, the class will continue to vote on the read-aloud and shortly they will read their number-one selection.

7 Tally the votes. Announce and celebrate the winning title!

8 While reading aloud the class choice, add another title or two to the book basket and repeat the procedure. While the class is enjoying their choice of a teacher read-aloud, the children can be browsing the book basket for their vote.

9 Note that children might request a title from the book basket to read during self-selected reading time. By all means, allow borrowing from the book basket. However, remind children that if they read a title from the basket that is later selected as a read-aloud, those who already enjoyed the title want to stay "mum" and not ruin the title for those who have not read it.

Extension

- Having the teacher and class share in the read-aloud is a very motivating adaptation of Vote for the Read-Aloud. Try this extension by inviting children to select titles for the book basket, conduct the book talks, and share the read-aloud. This adaptation can be easily managed by placing children in small groups rotating Vote for the Read-Aloud throughout the class. Such an ongoing rotation allows all the children to participate in this adaptation several times during the school year.

- Vote for the Read-Aloud is also the perfect time to model that not all text is read the same way. Teachers can use the basket book talks to model and discuss different purposes for reading. For example, the teacher might explain that only a few poems from an anthology or several chapters from an informational text will be shared aloud (if voted the favorite) and then the book will be made available to the class for self-selection.

- Vote for the Read-Aloud can be extended by promoting a particular genre for a short period of time (e.g., a basket of all poetry, all magazine articles).
- Have building VIPs (principal, guidance counselor, school nurse, etc.) contribute titles to the book basket. Invite the building VIPs to provide a book talk for their title.
- Post the class read-aloud favorites on a *Wall of Fame* (see Chapter 21). Periodically discuss the text (type and topics) that the class is enjoying. During this discussion, help children make connections between the texts. For example, talk about the similarities and differences between a favorite fiction book about owls and an informational book about owls that the class selected.

.... **30** ....

Promoting the Value
of Literacy at Home

Promoting the Value of Literacy at Home provides a number of ideas that you can share with parents or guardians to foster their children's value of reading and writing.

Focus on Motivation and Literacy Learning

Home experiences play a significant role in children's literacy motivation. It is in the home that children learn authentic ways that reading and writing are integrated into life outside of school. You can increase parents' awareness of how they can foster their child's value of literacy by sharing one or more of the ideas presented here. Many of these ideas can benefit children's literacy learning by giving them additional practice in reading and writing for authentic purposes.

How It Works

Share one or more of the following ideas during parent–teacher conferences or in your classroom/school newsletter:

◆ *Get caught in the act of reading and writing.* When children see adults reading different types of texts and for different purposes (e.g., reading a novel, magazine, newspaper, online article, the mail, directions to build or repair something, recipes, coupons, telephone book, maps), they learn the different uses of reading and perceive that reading is a valuable activity. Similarly, when children see adults writing for multiple purposes (e.g., writing e-mails, thank-you notes, checks, reminder lists, filling in calendars with appointments, and journal writing), they see firsthand the importance and value of writing. The next time your child sees you reading or writing at home, know that you're having a positive influence on your child's literacy motivation!

◆ *Enjoy reading books with your child and discussing what you've read.* It is the nurturing aspect of parent–child reading that fosters positive reading motivation. When the experiences are pleasurable, your child will value this time together and develop lifelong, positive associations with reading. Consider asking your child questions about the book that are truly interesting before, during, and after reading. Arouse your child's curiosity and listen closely to what your child has to say. Recall experiences together that you're reminded of during the read-aloud or shared reading. Make reading a bonding experience with your child.

◆ *Share books with your child in different ways.* Most children can comprehend books read aloud to them that are too difficult for them to decode. If a book is too difficult for your child to read and you think he or she is interested in the book, please read the book aloud to your child. If the book is easy for him or her to read, your child may read aloud to you or you could take turns reading. Other possibilities include listening to books on CD/tape together or reading the same book independently and discussing it. And, remember—it's okay to put down a book if your child becomes uninterested.

◆ *Honor all print.* If your child is interested in reading comic books, magazines about automobiles, or jokes and riddles, please encourage your child to do so. When we read texts that are of interest to us, we find value in reading. Not allowing children to read texts of interest can negatively affect their motivation to read.

◆ *Visit the public library.* Libraries are valuable resources! They provide a wide range of books, books on CD, and magazines that you and your child can skim to find reading of interest. But sometimes libraries can be overwhelming. Encourage your child to tell the librarian about favorite topics or genres. The librarian can make recommendations, and your child can pick from among his or her suggestions. Join in the fun and check out some books for yourself! Also, consider participating in some of the programs libraries offer to you and your child.

◆ *Use writing at times to communicate with your child.* Place a note to your child in his or her lunchbox. Consider keeping a spiral bound "Kitchen Journal" that is kept on the table or counter for easy access. You can write notes to your child there and your child can respond (e.g., "Do you have practice after school today?" or "Clean your room!"). You may want to keep the journals over the years, noting how the Kitchen Journal "conversations" change as your child matures and grows as a writer. By communicating in writing, your child not only learns the value of writing, he or she is practicing reading and writing for an authentic purpose! This can have a positive impact on literacy learning and motivation.

◆ *Be careful about using extrinsic rewards to motivate your child to read or write*. Extrinsic rewards are incentives that are unrelated to the activity. So, for example, telling a child that he will get a pizza when he finishes reading a book is an attempt to motivate using an extrinsic reward. (Pizza is unrelated to reading.) Instead, consider fostering your child's intrinsic motivation to read and write by using some of the ideas described above. If you do reward, consider rewarding with something related to literacy (e.g., a magazine of interest, new pens or pencils, a new journal). That way, if your child tends to value the reward, he or she will value something related to reading and writing—and not pizza!

For more ideas, see *Rewarding Reading* (Chapter 27).

PART FOUR

Against All Odds

A Case Study of Small Changes and Big Differences

The call came in mid-September. Bill, a friend and outstanding elementary building principal, was requesting help. He was very concerned about the literacy communities (or lack thereof) in his two fifth-grade classrooms. He had done several observations and noticed that the students were very reluctant to read and talk about books. Being reluctant to read in fifth grade wasn't all that surprising given what we know about the erosion of motivation as students move through the elementary grades. The shocking concern was his report of silent classrooms. These were fifth graders! They should be talking all the time—even about books they might have been reluctant to read. This at an age known for being highly verbal and not without opinions. By the end of a 15-minute conversation we were just as concerned. Vowing to help, we arranged a meeting with his fifth-grade team.

In that meeting, we found a group of teachers frustrated by rigid, uniform expectations. The group, comprised of two fifth-grade classroom teachers, two reading specialists, a learning support teacher, and Bill, realized that their instruction was doing little to nurture intrinsic reading motivation. They wanted their students to read independently and widely, engage in discussions about text, and collaborate about books. At the same time, they understood their professional responsibility to provide standards-based lessons that prepared their students for high-stakes assessments. They wondered if standards-based instruction and motivating literacy practices were hopelessly at odds. "Can we arrange motivating literacy opportunities while delivering the mandated curriculum?" they asked. Or, as one teacher wondered, "Could we identify curricular considerate motivating practices?" (Marinak, in press). This inquiry led to an action research endeavor whereby we sought to nurture intrinsically motivated reading.

First Steps: Assessing and Studying

We decided that the first steps in what was sure to be a year-long journey was to consult the research about elementary reading motivation. We, the university professors on the team, suggested several studies to get started. The team read several of our investigations (Marinak & Gambrell, 2010; Mazzoni, Gambrell, & Korkeamaki, 1999) as well as research by Eccles, Wigfield, and their colleagues (Eccles, 1983; Eccles, Wigfield, Harold, & Blumenfeld, 1993; Wigfield & Eccles, 1992, 2000), Guthrie and his colleagues (Guthrie, 2010; Guthrie et al., 1996; Guthrie, Wigfield, & VonSecker, 2000), and Turner and Paris (1995). During discussion of the studies, it became clear that we needed to assess the current reading motivation of the 32 readers in the two fifth-grade classrooms. The group had become familiar and comfortable with the expectancy–value theory of motivation (Eccles, 1983). Consequently, the Motivation to Read Profile (MRP; Gambrell, Palmer, Codling, & Mazzoni, 1996), which is available in Part Five of this book, was the logical choice to assess the current needs of our readers. We used only the Reading Survey, a self-report, group-administered instrument for our pre- and postassessment measure.

The Reading Survey of the MRP contains 20 items that use a 1–4 Likert scale, with 4 representing the most positive response. Consistent with expectancy–value theory (Eccles, 1983), the 20-item survey assesses two specific dimensions of reading motivation: self-concept as a reader and value of reading. The items that focus on self-concept as a reader are designed to elicit information about students' self-perceived competence in reading and their self-perception relative to peers. The value of reading items elicit information about the value students place on reading tasks, particularly in terms of frequency of reading engagement and reading-related activities (Gambrell et al., 1996).

The preassessment data from the MRP indicated that self-concept about reading and value of reading were low in both classrooms when compared to two fifth-grade classrooms in another school district with similar demographics.

Taking Action: Small Changes

After reading the research and studying the MRP results, the group decided to take action. Echoing the words of our teacher collogue, could we identify curricular considerate motivating practices (Marinak, in press)? In other words, was it possible to implement small changes in practice that did not compromise the integrity of the standards-based instruction required in the district but make a big difference in the reading motivation of our students? The group spent several months strategizing about potential actions with implementation during the second semester of the school year (mid-January).

The options decided upon by the team were consistent with expectancy–value theory (Eccles, 1983) and the dimensions of reading motivation identified during our literature review. We were committed to offering as many choices as possible, as well as providing opportunities for collaboration, authenticity, and challenge

(Turner & Paris, 1995). The three methods selected were Vote for the Read-Aloud, Experts Teaching, and Book Clubs from Rewarding Reading. Here's how it worked.

Vote for the Read-Aloud

For the second semester of the school year, the fifth-grade teachers allowed their students to choose the teacher read-aloud. This decision was based on a perceived lack of enthusiasm for the teacher read-aloud as well as data from the MRP. MRP scores indicated that many students did not value the teacher read-aloud, especially the boys. When it was time for a new read-aloud, we gathered eight new books (four fiction and four nonfiction) in a basket. We book-talked each title and told students that they would have the opportunity to vote for their choice in 3 days. We encouraged students to "browse" the book basket until it was time to vote. During the 3 days from book talk to vote, we watched and listened. When the time came to vote, we asked students to complete a paper ballot indicating their number-one and number-two choices. Vote for the Read-Aloud was used for the remainder of the year.

Experts Teaching

During the spring semester, each fifth-grade classroom used three informational titles during reading instruction. In an effort to encourage student discussion, the team decided that a modified Jigsaw (Aronson, Blaney, Slephin, Sikes, & Snapp, 1978) could be used to chunk the titles (vs. traditional small-group instruction). Our goal was to encourage expertise within each group. Due to curricular constraints, it was not possible to allow the students to choose their group. However, an attempt was made to include choice, challenge, collaboration, and authenticity during Experts Teaching. The informational titles were authentic children's literature and believed to be of high interest for fifth-grade students, including *The Book of North American Owls* by Helen Rooney Sattler, and *Wolves* and *Tornadoes* by Seymour Simon.

Each group was assigned a chunk of the texts. In some cases, the chunk was a chapter. In books without chapters, we divided the book into logical chunks based on the content. The students in each group were encouraged to discuss and prioritize the information to be shared with peers. In addition, and perhaps most important, the groups negotiated how they were going to teach the information and subsequently collaborated to prepare the presentation.

Book Clubs

Book Clubs were added because the classroom teachers overheard their students complain about independent reading time, referring to SSR as "sit down, shut up, and read." In an effort to provide students with additional opportunities for choice and collaboration about books, the fifth-grade teachers suspended traditional self-selected reading for the final 9 weeks of the year and replaced it with Book Clubs. With the support of the reading specialists and learning support teacher, they were able to offer five Book Clubs: three fiction titles, a nonfiction title, and a current-events group that accessed news from the Internet. After the teachers provided a brief overview of the options, each student selected a Book Club. On Mondays, Wednesdays, and Fridays during self-selected reading time, students read their books or articles. On Tuesdays and Thursdays, the Book Clubs met to discuss their reading.

Big Differences

So what happened as a result of our efforts? Evaluation of the motivation practices was twofold. First, like our students, we kept the dialogue active within our team. Everyone kept a reflection journal, jotting quick notes about behaviors and conversations. In addition, the group had ongoing conversations in person during monthly meetings and electronically in shared e-mails. Second, we conducted a postassessment of reading motivation using the MRP.

Reflections

Both teachers reported that students listen attentively and asked questions during their Vote for the Read-Aloud book talks. In addition, everyone on the team noticed the students regularly browsing the book basket during the 3 days leading up to the vote. Interestingly, both teachers described what they called "book lobbying" in the days before the vote. They heard students "lobbying" each other for book votes (e.g., "If you vote for my number-one choice this time, I'll vote for yours next time"). Both teachers also documented that following the read-aloud vote, the books not selected were consistently borrowed by students and read during independent reading. In fact, this phenomenon prompted what the teachers described as a "spontaneous confidentiality discussion" in both classrooms. When students realized the book basket titles were being read by their peers and might later be a class choice, they asked each other not to "spoil the book" if it was voted a read-aloud (Marinak, in press).

Reflections regarding Experts Teaching revealed high levels of on-task behavior and engaged discussion. One example of this enthusiasm was that students from both classrooms frequently asked to work on their presentation during recess or after completing other reading workshop assignments. At the conclusion of their expert group meetings, we enjoyed a wide variety of presentation modes, including plays, games, PowerPoints, posters, and videos. In addition to markedly more conversation, we recorded evidence of increased value of reading. One example, as noted in the introduction of Experts Teaching, is that the title of this modified Jigsaw (Aronson et al., 1978) came from Aaron. One day he asked us what "this" (working in groups and teaching each other) was called. But before we could respond, Aaron quickly offered that he knew. "It's called experts teaching, right? We are becoming experts, and we are teaching." Hence, our collaborations using informational text became forever known as "experts teaching" (Marinak, in press).

The Book Clubs were also well received. Perhaps the best anecdotal evidence of increasing motivation was that our classroom teachers quickly realized that their leadership was not necessary. In fact, during a team meeting, one of the fifth-grade teachers said, "They didn't need me at all. They couldn't wait to talk to each other about their reading" (Marinak, in press).

Postassessment of Motivation

The postassessment administration of the MRP revealed what we suspected throughout the spring semester. When compared to both the groups' preassessment MRP scores and the two fifth-grade classrooms used as a control group, our fifth graders self-reported significantly higher total reading motivation scores. Interestingly, when examining the two subscales of the MRP, there were no differences between our fifth graders and the control classrooms with respect to self-concept as a reader. However, when compared to students in the control classrooms, our fifth-grade students reported that they valued reading more after the three small changes implemented by the team. In other words, this finding suggests that Vote for the Teacher Read-Aloud, Experts Teaching, and Book Clubs resulted in higher value of reading when compared to fifth-grade peers who did not participate in similar motivation opportunities.

Concluding Thoughts

At the conclusion of the year, the team agreed that small changes could result in big motivational differences. We felt confident (and the statewide assessment data indicated) that we had identified curricular-considerate practices. Our attempts to maximize reading motivation using choice, authenticity, challenge, and collaboration appeared to be effective for this group of fifth graders. However, knowing that intrinsic reading motivation is idiosyncratic, the team realized that nurturing engaged readers in the future will surely be a nomadic journey. There is no doubt that the conversations started during this case study will continue for many years to come. But what exciting conversations they will be!

References

Aronson, E., Blaney, N., Stephin, C., Sikes, J., & Snapp, M. (1978). *The jigsaw classroom.* Beverly Hills, CA: Sage.

Eccles, J. (1983). Expectancies, value, and academic behaviors. In J. T. Spence (Ed.), *Achievement and achievement motives* (pp. 75–146). San Francisco: Freeman.

Eccles, J., Wigfield, A., Harold, R., & Blumenfeld, P. (1993). Age and gender differences in children's self- and task perceptions during elementary school. *Child Development, 64,* 830–847.

Gambrell, L., Palmer, B., Codling, R., & Mazzoni. S. (1996). Assessing motivation to read. *The Reading Teacher, 49*(7), 518–533.

Guthrie, J. (2010). Contexts for engagement and motivation in reading. Retrieved from *http://readingonline.org.*

Guthrie, J., Van Meter, P., McCann, A., Wigfield, A., Bender, L., Poundstone, C., et al. (1996). Growth of literacy engagement: Changes in motivations and strategies during concept-oriented reading instruction. *Reading Research Quarterly, 31*, 306–325.

Guthrie, J., Wigfield, A., & VonSecker, C. (2000). Effects of integrated instruction on motivation and strategy use in reading. *Journal of Educational Psychology, 92*(2), 331–341.

Marinak, B. (in press). Courageous reading instruction: The effects of an elementary motivation intervention. *Journal of Educational Research.*

Marinak, B., & Gambrell, L. (2010). Reading motivation: Exploring the elementary gender gap. *Literacy Research and Instruction, 49*(2), 129–141.

Mazzoni, S. A., Gambrell, L. B., & Korkeamaki, R. L. (1999, July–September). A cross cultural perspective of early literacy motivation. *Reading Psychology, 20*(3), 237–253.

Turner, J., & Paris, S. (1995). How literacy tasks influence children's motivation for literacy. *The Reading Teacher, 48*(8), 662–673.

Assessing Motivation
Instruments

In order to maximize motivation in your classroom, it is helpful to assess the literacy motivation of your students. This section of our book contains several assessment tools. Expectancy–value theory (Eccles, 1983) served as the theoretical model for the Motivation to Read Profile (Gambrell, Palmer, Codling, & Mazzoni, 1996) and the Motivation to Write Scale (Codling, Gambrell, Kennedy, Palmer, & Graham, 1996). This section also offers the Honor All Print Survey. Given the nature of assessing intrinsic motivation, all three tools are self-report instruments.

The Motivation to Read Profile (MRP) measures existing reading motivation. The MRP consists of two instruments: the Reading Survey (Form A) and the Conversational Interview (Form B). The Reading Survey assesses two specific dimensions of reading motivation—self-concept as a reader and value of reading. A scoring sheet for the Reading Survey is provided in Form C. The Conversational Interview provides information about the individual nature of students' reading motivation, such as what books and what stories are most interesting, favorite authors, and where and how children locate reading materials that interest them. Each subscale of the Reading Survey contains 10 items. Internal consistency was calculated for the two subscales. Cronbach's alpha revealed a moderately high reliability for both subscales of the MRP (self-concept = .75; value = .82). The MRP and the article in which this instrument was originally published are available in this section for your use.

The Motivation to Write Scale (MWS) assesses existing writing motivation. The MWS also consists of two instruments: the Writing Scale (Form D) and the Student Interview (Form E). The Writing Scale assesses two specific dimensions of writing motivation—self-concept as a writer and value of writing. The Self-Concept as a Writer subscale of the Writing Scale contains 12 items and the Value of Writing subscale contains 14 items. The Student Interview provides information about the individual nature of students' writing motivation, such as what do you write, how do you make writing better, and who gets you excited about writing. A scoring rubric for student interviews is presented in Form F. The complete MWS and portions of the National Reading Research Center Reading Research Report in which this tool was originally published are available in this section for your use.

The Honor All Print Survey (HAP; Form G) is an interest inventory that attempts to honor all print by inquiring about a wide variety of reading options—options students may not discuss unless specifically asked. The survey contains two multiple-choice questions and eight open-ended questions. The HAP is designed to give students the opportunity to comment on types of text not included on other interest inventories such as fact/list books, graphic novels, comic books, newspapers, magazines, and reading on the Internet. The HAP can be used a conversational interview with the results recorded by the teacher, or students can complete it independently. The HAP can provide important information about what students really like to read. The HAP is available at the end of this section for your use.

References

Codling, R. M., Gambrell, L. B., Kennedy, E., Palmer, B. M., & Graham, M. (1996). *The teacher, the text, and the context: Factors that influence elementary students' motivation to write* (Reading Research Report No. 59). College Park, MD: National Reading Research Center.

Eccles, J. (1983). Expectancies, values, and academic behaviors. In T. Spence (Ed.), *Achievement and achievement motives: Psychological and sociological approaches* (pp. 75–114). San Fransisco: Freeman.

Gambrell, L. B., Palmer, B. M., Codling, R. M., & Mazzoni, S. A. (1996). Assessing motivation to read. *The Reading Teacher, 49*(7), 518–533.

Assessing Motivation to Read
The Motivation to Read Profile

Teachers have long recognized that motivation is at the heart of many of the pervasive problems we face in teaching young children to read. In a study conducted by Veenman (1984), teachers ranked motivating students as one of their primary and overriding concerns. A more recent national survey of teachers also revealed that "creating interest in reading" was rated as the most important area for future research (O'Flahavan, Gambrell, Guthrie, Stahl, & Alvermann, 1992). The value teachers place on motivation is supported by a robust research literature that documents the link between motivation and achievement (Elley, 1992; Gambrell & Morrow, 1996; Guthrie, Schafer, Wang, & Afflerbach, 1993; Purves & Beach, 1972; Walberg & Tsai, 1985; Wixson & Lipson, 1991). The results of these studies clearly indicate the need to increase our understanding of how children acquire the motivation to develop into active, engaged readers.

Highly motivated readers are self-determining and generate their own reading opportunities. They want to read and choose to read for a wide range of personal reasons such as curiosity, involvement, social interchange, and emotional satisfaction. According to Guthrie (1996), highly motivated readers generate their own literacy learning opportunities, and in doing so they begin to determine their own destiny as literacy learners.

Research supports the notion that literacy learning is influenced by a variety of motivational factors (Deci & Ryan, 1985; Eccles, 1983; Ford, 1992; Kuhl, 1986; Lepper, 1988; Maehr, 1976; McCombs, 1991; Wigfield, 1994). A number of current theories suggest that self-perceived competence and task value are major determinants of motivation and task engagement. For example, Eccles (1983) advanced an "expectancy–value" theory of motivation that states that motivation is strongly influ-

This chapter is an adapted version of Gambrell, L. B., Palmer, B. M., Codling, R. M., & Mazzoni, S. A. (1996), *The Reading Teacher, 49*(7), 518–533. Copyright 1996 by the International Reading Association/John Wiley & Sons, Inc. Adapted by permission.

enced by one's expectation of success or failure at a task, as well as by the "value" or relative attractiveness the individual places on the task. The expectancy component of Eccles's theory is supported by a number of research studies that suggest that students who believe they are capable and competent readers are more likely to outperform those who do not hold such beliefs (Paris & Oka, 1986; Schunk, 1985). In addition, students who perceive reading as valuable and important and who have personally relevant reasons for reading will engage in reading in a more planned and effortful manner (Ames & Archer, 1988; Dweck & Elliott, 1983; Paris & Oka, 1986).

The work of other motivational theorists, such as Ford (1992) and Winne (1985), has been grounded in the expectancy–value theory. Ford's (1992) motivational systems theory maintains that people will attempt to attain goals they value and perceive as achievable. Similarly, Winne (1985) views the "idealized reader" as one who feels competent and perceives reading as being of personal value and practical importance. Within this theoretical framework, reading motivation is defined by an individual's self-concept and the value the individual places on reading. Evidence from theory and research supports the notion that high motivation to read is associated with positive self-concept and high value assignment, while low motivation to read is associated with poor self-concept as a reader and low value assignment (Ford, 1992; Henk & Melnick, 1995; Wigfield, 1994). Given the emphasis on self-concept and task value in motivation theory, it seems important that teachers have resources for assessing both of these factors.

A review of current instruments designed to assess reading motivation revealed a number of instruments for measuring students' general attitude toward reading (e.g., McKenna & Kear, 1990; Tunnell, Calder, Justen, & Phaup, 1988), as well as several that measure the specific dimension of self-concept (Harter, 1981; Henk & Melnick, 1995; Pintrich & DeGroot, 1990). Henk and Melnick's (1995) instrument, the Reader Self-Perception Scale, was "developed in response to calls in the professional literature for self-evaluation instruments that measure the way readers appraise themselves" (p. 471). The instrument described in this chapter extends the work of Henk and Melnick by assessing two fundamental components of motivation suggested by motivational theory: self-concept and task value. In addition, none of the existing instruments combine quantitative and qualitative approaches for assessing reading motivation. Our purpose was to develop a public-domain instrument that would provide teachers with an efficient and reliable way to quantitatively and qualitatively assess reading motivation by evaluating students' self-concept as readers and the value they place on reading. This chapter presents the Motivation to Read Profile (MRP), along with a discussion of its development and suggestions for its use with elementary students.

Description of the MRP

The MRP consists of two basic instruments: the Reading Survey and the Conversational Interview. The Reading Survey is a self-report, group-administered instrument, and the Conversational Interview is designed for individual administration. The survey assesses two specific dimensions of reading motivation, self-concept as a reader and value of reading; the interview provides information about the individual nature of students' reading motivation, such as what books and stories are most interesting, favorite authors, and where and how children locate reading materials that interest them most. Figure 1 profiles the two instruments.

Because the MRP combines information from a group-administered survey instrument with an individual interview, it provides a useful tool for exploring more fully the personal dimensions of students' reading motivation. The MRP is highly individualized, which makes it particularly appropriate for inclusion in portfolio assessment.

The Reading Survey

This instrument consists of 20 items and uses a 4-point response scale (see Form A). The survey assesses two specific dimensions of reading motivation: self-concept as a reader (10 items) and value of reading (10 items). The items that focus on self-concept as a reader are designed to elicit information about students' self-perceived competence in reading and self-perceived performance relative to peers. The value of reading items are designed to elicit information about the value students place on reading tasks and activities, particularly in terms of frequency of engagement and reading-related activities.

The Conversational Interview

The interview is made up of three sections (see Form B). The first section probes motivational factors related to the reading of narrative text (three questions); the second section elicits information about informational reading (three questions); and the final section focuses on more general factors related to reading motivation (eight questions).

The interview is designed to initiate an informal, conversational exchange between the teacher and the student. According to Burgess (1980), conversational

Reading Survey	Conversational Interview
• Group administration	• Individual administration
• 15–20 minutes to administer	• 15–20 minutes to administer
• 20 items	• 14 scripted items
• Cued response	• Open-ended free response
• Subscales:	• Sections:
Self-Concept as a Reader	Narrative reading
Value of Reading	Informational reading
	General reading

FIGURE 1. Instruments of the MRP.

interviews are social events that can provide greater depth of understanding than more rigid interview techniques. Although conversational interviews are scripted, deviations from the script are anticipated and expected (Baker, 1984). The teacher is encouraged to deviate from the basic script in order to glean information that might otherwise be missed or omitted in a more formal, standardized interview approach. Teachers need to keep in mind that the primary purpose of the conversational interview is to generate information that will provide authentic insights into students' reading experiences. Participating in a conversational interview allows children to use their unique ways of describing their reading motivation and experiences and to raise ideas and issues related to personal motivation that may not be reflected in the scripted interview items (Denzin, 1970).

How Was the MRP Developed?

Item selection for the MRP was based on a review of research and theories related to motivation and included an analysis of existing instruments designed to assess motivation and attitude toward reading. A number of instruments were examined in order to gather ideas for the development of an initial pool of MRP items (Gottfried, 1986; Harter, 1981; Johnson & Gaskins, 1991; McKenna & Kear, 1990; Pintrich & DeGroot, 1990; Raynor & Nochajski, 1986; Schell, 1992; Tunnell et al., 1988).

An assessment instrument is useful only if it is valid and reliable. *Validity* refers to the instrument's ability to measure the trait it purports to measure, and *reliability* refers to the ability of the instrument to consistently measure that trait. To gain information about the validity and reliability of the MRP, the Reading Survey and the Conversational Interview were field-tested.

Development and Field Testing of the Reading Survey

The criteria for item selection and development for the survey instrument included (1) applicability to grades 2 through 6, (2) applicability to all teaching approaches and materials, (3) suitability for group administration, and (4) accuracy in reflecting the appropriate dimension of motivation (i.e., self-concept or value). All survey items employ a 4-point response scale to avoid neutral, central response patterns. A 4-point scale also seemed more appropriate for elementary students as there is some evidence to suggest that young children have difficulty simultaneously discriminating among more than five discrete categories (Case & Khanna, 1981; Nitko, 1983). In order to avoid repetition in the presentation of the response alternatives and to control for the threat of "response set" (i.e., children selecting the same responses for each item), some response alternatives proceed from most positive to least positive while others are ordered in the opposite way.

An initial pool of survey items was developed based on the criteria described above. Three experienced classroom teachers, who were also graduate students in reading, critiqued over 100 items for their construct validity in assessing students' self-concept or value of reading. We compiled the items that received 100% agreement. These items were then submitted to four classroom teachers who were asked to sort the items into three categories: measures self-concept, measures value of reading, not sure or questionable. Only those items that received 100% trait agreement were selected for inclusion on the Reading Survey instrument used in the field testing.

The final version of the Reading Survey instrument was administered in the late fall and early spring with 330 third- and fifth-grade students in 27 classrooms in four schools from two school districts in an eastern U.S. state. To determine whether the traits measured by the Reading Survey (Self-Concept as a Reader and Value of Reading) corresponded to the two subscales, factor analyses were conducted using the unweighted least squares method and a varimax rotation. Only items that loaded cleanly on the two traits were included in the final instrument. To assess the internal consistency of the Reading Survey, Cronbach's (1951) alpha statistic was calculated, which revealed a moderately high reliability for both subscales (self-concept = .75; value = .82). In addition, pre- and posttest reliability coefficients were calculated for the subscales (self-concept = .68; value = .70), which confirmed the moderately high reliability of the instrument.

Development and Field Testing of the Conversational Interview

Approximately 60 open-ended questions regarding narrative and informational reading, general and specific reading experiences, and home and school reading practices were developed for the initial pool of interview items. These items were field-tested in the spring with a stratified random sample of 48 students (24 third graders and 24 fifth graders). Classroom teachers identified students as at grade level, above grade level, or below grade level. The teachers were then asked to identify, within each of the three ability-level lists, the two most "highly motivated readers" and the two "least motivated readers." Twenty-four students from the list of most highly motivated readers and 24 students from the list of least motivated readers participated in the field testing of the 60 interview items. Two graduate students, who were former classroom teachers, analyzed the 48 student protocols and selected 14 questions that revealed the most useful information about students' motivation to read. These 14 questions were used for the final version of the Conversational Interview.

Validity and Reliability of the MRP

Additional steps were taken to validate the final version of the MRP. Responses to the survey and conversational interview were examined for consistency of information across the two instruments. The survey and interview responses of two highly motivated and two less motivated readers were randomly selected for analysis. Two independent raters compared each student's responses on the survey instrument and the interview. For example, one item on the survey asks the students to indicate whether they think they are a "very good reader," "good reader," "OK reader," or "poor reader." Comments made during the conversational interview were analyzed to determine if students provided any confirming evidence about their self-perceived competence in reading.

Two raters independently compared each student's responses to items on the survey with information provided during the interview, with an interrater agreement of .87. There was consistent, supporting information in the interview responses for approximately 70% of the information tapped in the survey instrument. The results of these data analyses support the notion that the children responded consistently on both types of assessment instruments (survey, interview) and across time (fall, spring).

A further test of the validity of the Reading Survey explored the relationship between level of motivation and reading achievement. Motivational theory and research indicate a positive correlation between motivation and achievement (Ford, 1992; McKenna & Kear, 1990). Teachers categorized students as having low, average, or high reading performance. Statistically significant differences were found among the mean scores on the self-concept measure for high, middle, and low reading achievement groups, revealing that scores were positively associated with level of reading achievement. In addition, statistically significant differences were found between mean scores of third- and fifth-grade students on the value measure, with younger students scoring more positively than older students. This finding is in keeping with the work of other researchers who have found that positive attitude toward reading decreases as children progress through the elementary grades (e.g., McKenna & Kear, 1990).

Administering the MRP

The MRP combines group and individual assessment procedures. The Reading Survey instrument can be administered to an entire class, to a small group, or to an individual, while the Conversational Interview is designed to be conducted on an individual basis.

Administration and Scoring of the Reading Survey

The administration of the Reading Survey instrument takes approximately 15–20 minutes (see Figure 2). Teachers should consider grade level and attention span when deciding how and when to administer it. For example, teachers of young children may decide to administer the first 10 items in one session and the final 10 during a second session.

The survey is designed to be read aloud to students. One of the problems inherent in much of the motivational research is that reading ability often confounds the results so that proficient, higher ability readers are typically identified as "motivated," while less proficient, lower ability readers are identified as "unmotivated." This characterization is inaccurate; there are proficient readers who are not highly

Distribute copies of the Reading Survey. Ask students to write their names on the space provided.

Say:
    I am going to read some sentences to you. I want to know how you feel about your reading. There are no right or wrong answers. I really want to know how you honestly feel about reading.
    I will read each sentence twice. Do not mark your answer until I tell you to. The first time I read the sentence I want you to think about the best answer for you. The second time I read the sentence I want you to fill in the space beside your best answer. Mark only one answer. Remember: Do not mark your answer until I tell you to. OK, let's begin.

Read the first sample item. Say:
Sample 1: I am in (pause) first grade, (pause) second grade, (pause) third grade, (pause) fourth grade, (pause) fifth grade, (pause) sixth grade.

Read the first sample again. Say:
This time as I read the sentence, mark the answer that is right for you. I am in (pause) first grade, (pause) second grade, (pause) third grade, (pause) fourth grade, (pause) fifth grade, (pause) sixth grade.

Read the second sample item. Say:
Sample 2: I am a (pause) boy, (pause) girl.

Say: Now, get ready to mark your answer.
I am a (pause) boy, (pause) girl.

Read the remaining items in the same way (e.g., number_____, sentence stem followed by a pause, each option followed by a pause, and then give specific directions for students to mark their answers while you repeat the entire item).

FIGURE 2. Teacher directions for the MRP Reading Survey.

motivated to read, just as there are less proficient readers who are highly motivated to read (McCombs, 1991; Roettger, 1980). When students are instructed to independently read and respond to survey items, the results for the less proficient, lower ability readers may not be reliable due to their frustration when reading the items. For these reasons, the Reading Survey is designed to be read aloud by the teacher to help ensure the veracity of student responses.

Students must understand that their responses to the survey items will not be graded. They should be told that the results of the survey will provide information that the teacher can use to make reading more interesting for them and that the information will be helpful only if they provide their most honest responses.

Directions for scoring the Reading Survey (see Figure 3) and a scoring sheet (see Form C) are provided. When scoring the survey, the most positive response is assigned the highest number (4) while the least positive response is assigned the lowest number (1). For example, if a student reported that he or she is a "good" reader, a "3" would be recorded. Teachers can compute percentage scores on the entire Reading Survey or on the two subscales (Self-Concept as a Reader and Value of Reading). Space is also provided at the bottom of the scoring sheet for the teacher

The survey has 20 items based on a 4-point scale. The highest total score possible is 80 points. On some items the response options are ordered least positive to most positive (see item 2 below), with the least positive response option having a value of 1 point and the most positive option having a point value of 4. On other items, however, the response options are reversed (see item 1 below). In those cases it will be necessary to recode the response options. Items where recoding is required are starred on the scoring sheet.

Example: Here is how Maria completed items 1 and 2 on the Reading Survey.

1. My friends think I am _____.
   □ a very good reader
   ■ a good reader
   □ an OK reader
   □ a poor reader

2. Reading a book is something I like to do.
   □ Never
   □ Not very often
   □ Sometimes
   ■ Often

To score item 1 it is first necessary to recode the response options so that

   a poor reader equals 1 point,

   an OK reader equals 2 points,

   a good reader equals 3 points, and

   a very good reader equals 4 points.

Since Maria answered that she is a good reader the point value for that item, 3, is entered on the first line of the Self-Concept column on the scoring sheet. See below.

    The response options for item 2 are ordered least positive (1 point) to most positive (4 points), so scoring item 2 is easy. Simply enter the point value associated with Maria's response. Because Maria selected the fourth option, a 4 is entered for item 2 under the Value of Reading column on the scoring sheet. See below.

Scoring Sheet

Self-Concept as a Reader	Value of Reading
*recode 1.<u>3</u>	2.<u>4</u>

To calculate the Self-Concept raw score and Value raw score add all student responses in the respective column. The Full Survey raw score is obtained by combining the column raw scores. To convert the raw scores to percentage scores, divide student raw scores by the total possible score (40 for each subscale, 80 for the full survey).

FIGURE 3. Scoring directions for the MRP Reading Survey.

to note any interesting or unusual responses that might be probed later during the Conversational Interview.

Administration of the Conversational Interview

The Conversational Interview is designed to elicit information that will help the teacher gain a deeper understanding of a student's reading motivation in an informal, conversational manner (see Figure 4). The entire interview takes approximately 15–20 minutes, but it can easily be conducted in three 5- to 7-minute sessions, one for each of the three sections of the interview (narrative, informational, and general reading). Individual portfolio conferences are an ideal time to conduct the interview.

We suggest that teachers review student responses on the Reading Survey prior to conducting the Conversational Interview so that they may contemplate and anticipate possible topics to explore. During the Conversational Interview, some children will talk enthusiastically without probing, but others may need support and encouragement. Children who are shy or who tend to reply in short, quick answers can be encouraged to elaborate upon their responses through nonthreatening phrases like "Tell me more about that . . . ," "What else can you tell me . . . ?," and "Why do you think that . . . ?". Probing of brief responses from children is often necessary in order to reveal important and relevant information.

Teachers are also encouraged to extend, modify, and adapt the 14 questions outlined in the Conversational Interview, especially during conversations with individual students. Follow-up questions based on students' comments often provide the most significant information in such an interview.

---

1. Duplicate the Conversational Interview so that you have a form for each child.
2. Choose in advance the section(s) or specific questions you want to ask from the Conversational Interview. Reviewing the information on students' Reading Surveys may provide information about additional questions that could be added to the interview.
3. Familiarize yourself with the basic questions provided in the interview prior to the interview session in order to establish a more conversational setting.
4. Select a quiet corner of the room and a calm period of the day for the interview.
5. Allow ample time for conducting the Conversational Interview.
6. Follow up on interesting comments and responses to gain a fuller understanding of students' reading experiences.
7. Record students' responses in as much detail as possible. If time and resources permit, you may want audiotape answers to A1 and B1 to be transcribed after the interview for more in-depth analysis.
8. Enjoy this special time with each student!

FIGURE 4. Teacher directions for the MRP Conversational Interview.

Using the Results of the MRP to Make Instructional Decisions

Information from the results of the MRP can be used to plan instructional activities that will support students' reading development. The following list provides some ideas for ways in which the results can be used to enhance literacy learning. First, specific recommendations are presented for using the results of the Reading Survey and the Conversational Interview. Then, general recommendations for using the MRP are provided.

Using the Results of the Reading Survey

- ◆ Because of the highly individualized nature of motivation, careful examination of an individual's responses may provide valuable insights that can be used to create more meaningful, motivational contexts for reading instruction. For example, if a child indicates on the survey form that "reading is very hard" and that "reading is boring," the teacher can suggest books of particular interest to the child that the child can read with ease.

- ◆ A total score and separate scores on the two subscales of the Reading Survey (Self-Concept as a Reader and Value of Reading) can be computed for each student. Teachers can then identify those children who have lower scores in these areas. These students may be the ones who are in need of additional support in developing motivation to read and may benefit from interventions to promote reading engagement.

- ◆ Students who have lower subscores on the Self-Concept as a Reader scale may benefit from experiences that highlight successful reading. For example, to build feelings of competence, the teacher can arrange for the child to read books to children in lower grades.

- ◆ Students who have lower subscores on the Value of Reading scale may benefit from experiences that emphasize meaningful purposes for reading. For example, the teacher can ask the child to read about how to care for a class pet or involve the child in class plays or skits.

- ◆ If many children score low on the Value of Reading scale, the teacher can implement meaningful cooperative group activities where children teach one another about what they have read regarding a particular topic. The teacher can also involve the class in projects that require reading instructions, for example, preparing a recipe, creating a crafts project, or performing a science experiment.

- ◆ Class averages for the total score and subscores on the Reading Survey can be computed. This information may be helpful in obtaining an overview of the classroom level of motivation at various points throughout the school year.

- ◆ Teachers may also analyze class responses to an individual item on the Reading Survey. For example, if many children indicate that they seldom read at home, the teacher may decide to implement a home reading program, or the teacher might discuss the importance of home reading and parent involvement during parent night. Another survey item asks children to complete the following statement: "I think libraries are. . . ." If many students report a negative response toward libraries, the teacher can probe the class for further information in order to identify reasons, which can then be addressed.

Using the Results of the Conversational Interview

♦ The primary purpose of the Conversational Interview is to gain insight into what motivates the student to engage in reading. Therefore, the interview questions focus on reading that students find most interesting. This information can inform the teacher about specific topics, books, and authors that the individual student finds engaging and motivating.

♦ The Conversational Interview might also reveal particular activities related to reading that the child enjoys. For example, one child in our field study mentioned his father several times during the interview, talking about reading to his father, telling his father about something interesting he had read, and selecting and buying books with his father. In such a situation, a teacher can suggest home activities or even specific books that the father and child might enjoy reading at home.

♦ Class responses to items on the Conversational Interview may also reveal useful information. For example, if many children express interest in a particular topic, the teacher may find ways to include reading activities regarding the topic. If children express interest in a particular instructional activity, such as inviting guest readers into the classroom or "Young Authors' Night" where children present their stories to parents and guests, this information can then be taken into account for future planning.

General Recommendations for Using the MRP

♦ The MRP can provide a means of assessing, monitoring, and documenting student responses to innovations in the classroom that are designed to promote reading motivation. For example, the teacher might collect information using the MRP prior to and following the implementation of a reading motivational intervention, such as a sustained silent reading program or involvement in a classroom or a schoolwide reading motivational program.

♦ The MRP can be given at the beginning of the year to provide the teacher with profiles of each child. This information can be placed in children's reading portfolios. Teachers may decide to administer the MRP several times throughout the school year so that changes in the child's attitudes and interests about reading can be documented and compared.

♦ The MRP can be administered at each grade level and the assessment data retained so that teachers can compare changes in a child's self-concept as a reader and value of reading as he or she progresses from grade to grade.

These are only a sampling of ideas of the ways in which the MRP can be used in the classroom. Each teacher will have his or her own particular insights about ways in which the MRP information can best be applied to meet students' needs.

Cautions about Interpreting Responses to the MRP

Although there is support for the reliability and validity of the MRP, it is a self-report instrument, and so it has limitations that are commonly associated with such instruments. For example, it is impossible to determine from self-report instruments alone whether or not students actually feel, believe, or do the things they report. Even though the elaborate descriptive information gleaned from the interview can substantiate survey responses to some extent, only careful observation can verify information derived from the MRP.

Also, one should be cautious when interpreting responses to individual items due to the contextual nature of reading motivation. For example, a student might feel highly competent as a reader when reading high-interest, self-selected narrative materials and yet feel far less competent when reading content-area materials. It is more important to look across the survey and interview responses to determine patterns that reveal factors that are relevant to the student's reading motivation.

Finally, as with any assessment, the MRP should be used in conjunction with other assessment instruments, techniques, and procedures. Teachers should consider the MRP as one source of information about reading motivation.

Summary

Motivation is an integral component of reading instruction. In addition, a number of studies suggest a connection between motivation and achievement. Current motivational theory emphasizes the role of self-perceived competence and task value as determinants of motivation and task engagement. The MRP was developed to provide teachers with an efficient and reliable instrument for assessing reading motivation by evaluating students' self-concept as readers and the value they place on reading. In addition, the assessment instrument provides both quantitative and qualitative information by combining the use of a survey instrument and an individual interview.

There are a number of ways in which the MRP can be used to make instructional decisions. Teachers are in the best position to decide how they will apply the information gleaned from the MRP in their classrooms. Ideally, the MRP will help teachers acquire insights about individual students, particularly those students whom teachers worry most about in terms of their reading motivation and development. The individualized nature of the information derived from the MRP makes this instrument particularly appropriate for inclusion in portfolio assessment. Careful scrutiny of the responses to the Reading Survey and the Conversational Interview, coupled with teacher observations of student behaviors in various classroom reading contexts, can help teachers plan for meaningful instruction that will support students in becoming highly motivated readers.

Authors' Notes

We would like to thank the students, teachers, and principals in Charles and Frederick Counties, Maryland, for their support and assistance in the piloting and development of the instruments described here. The work reported here is a National Reading Research Project of the University of Georgia and University of Maryland. It was supported under the Educational Research Development Centers Program (PR/Award No. 117A20007) as administered by the Office of Educational Research and Improvement, U.S. Department of Education. The findings and opinions expressed here do not necessarily reflect the position or policies of the National Reading Research Center, the Office of Educational Research and Improvement, or the U.S. Department of Education.

References

Ames, C., & Archer, J. (1988). Achievement goals in the classroom: Students' learning strategies and motivation processes. *Journal of Educational Psychology, 80,* 260–267.

Baker, C. D. (1984). The search for adultness: Membership work in adolescent–adult talk. *Human Studies, 7,* 301–323.

Burgess, R. (1980). *Field research: A sourcebook and field manual.* London: Allen & Unwin.

Case, R., & Khanna, F. (1981). The missing links: Stages in children's progression from sensorimotor to logical thought. In K. W. Fischer (Ed.), *Cognitive development: New directions for child development* (pp. 21–32). San Francisco: Jossey-Bass.

Cronbach, L. J. (1951). Coefficient alpha and the internal structure of tests. *Psychometrika, 16,* 297–334.

Deci, E., & Ryan, R. (1985). *Intrinsic motivation and self determination in human behavior.* New York: Plenum Press.

Denzin, N. (1970). *The research act in sociology.* London: Butterworth.

Dweck, C., & Elliott, E. (1983). Achievement motivation. In E. M. Heatherington (Ed.), *Handbook of child psychology: Vol. 4. Socialization, personality, and social development* (pp. 643–691). New York: Wiley.

Eccles, J. (1983). Expectancies, values and academic behaviors. In J. T. Spence (Ed.), *Achievement and achievement motives* (pp. 75–146). San Francisco: Freeman.

Elley, W. B. (1992). *How in the world do students read?* Hamburg, Germany: International Association for the Evaluation of Educational Achievement.

Ford, M. E. (1992). *Motivating humans.* Newbury Park, CA: Sage.

Gambrell, L. B., & Morrow, L. M. (1996). Creating motivating contexts for literacy learning. In L. Baker, P. Afflerbach, & D. Reinking (Eds.), *Developing engaged readers in home and school communities* (pp. 115–136). Hillsdale, NJ: Erlbaum.

Gottfried, A. E. (1986). *Children's Academic Intrinsic Motivation Inventory.* Odessa, FL: Psychological Assessment Resources.

Guthrie, J. T. (1996). Educational contexts for engagement in literacy. *The Reading Teacher, 49*, 432–445.

Guthrie, J. T., Schafer, W., Wang, Y., & Afflerbach, P. (1993). *Influences of instruction on reading engagement: An empirical exploration of a social-cognitive framework of reading activity* (Research Report No. 3). Athens, GA: National Reading Research Center.

Harter, S. (1981). A new self-report scale of intrinsic versus extrinsic orientation in the classroom: Motivational and informational components. *Developmental Psychology, 77*, 300–312.

Henk, W., & Melnick, S. A. (1995). The Reader Self Perception Scale (RSPS): A new tool for measuring how children feel about themselves as readers. *The Reading Teacher, 48*, 470–482.

Johnson, C. S., & Gaskins, J. (1991). Reading attitude: Types of materials and specific strategies. *Reading Improvement, 28*, 237–242.

Kuhl, J. (1986). Introduction. In J. Kuhl & J. W. Atkinson (Eds.), *Motivation, thought, and action* (pp. 1–16). New York: Praeger.

Lepper, M. R. (1988). Motivational considerations in the study of instruction. *Cognition and Instruction, 5*, 289–309.

Maehr, M. L. (1976). Continuing motivation: An analysis of a seldom considered educational outcome. *Review of Educational Research, 46*, 443–462.

McCombs, B. L. (1991). Unraveling motivation: New perspectives from research and practice. *Journal of Experimental Education, 60*, 3–88.

McKenna, M. C., & Kear, D. J. (1990). Measuring attitude toward reading: A new tool for teachers. *The Reading Teacher, 43*, 626–639.

Nitko, A. J. (1983). *Educational tests and measurement: An introduction.* New York: Harcourt Brace Jovanovich.

O'Flahavan, J., Gambrell, L. B., Guthrie, J., Stahl, S., & Alvermann, D. (1992). Poll results guide activities of research center. *Reading Today, 10*, 12.

Paris, S. G., & Oka, E. R. (1986). Self-regulated learning among exceptional children. *Exceptional Children, 53*, 103–108.

Pintrich, P. R., & DeGroot, E. V. (1990). Motivational and self-regulated learning components of classroom academic performance. *Journal of Educational Psychology, 82*, 33–40.

Purves, A., & Beach, R. (1972). *Literature and the reader: Research on response to literature, reading interests, and teaching of literature.* Urbana, IL: National Council of Teachers of English.

Raynor, J. O., & Nochajski, T. H. (1986). Development of the motivation for particular activity scale. In D. R. Brown & I. Vernoff (Eds.), *Frontiers of motivational psychology* (pp. 1–25). New York: Springer-Verlag.

Roettger, D. (1980). Elementary students' attitudes toward reading. *The Reading Teacher, 33*, 451–453.

Schell, L. M. (1992). Student perceptions of good and poor readers. *Reading Improvement, 29*, 50–55.

Schunk, D. (1985). Self-efficacy and school learning. *Psychology in the Schools, 22*, 208–223.

Tunnell, M. O., Calder, J. E., Justen, J. E., & Phaup, E. S. (1988). Attitudes of young readers. *Reading Improvement, 25*, 237–242.

Veenman, S. (1984). Perceived problems of beginning teachers. *Review of Educational Research, 54,* 143–178.

Walberg, H. J., & Tsai, S. (1985). Correlates of reading achievement and attitude: A national assessment study. *Journal of Educational Research, 78,* 159–167.

Wigfield, A. (1994). Expectancy–value theory of achievement motivation: A developmental perspective. *Educational Psychology Review, 6*(1), 48–78.

Winne, P. (1985). Steps toward promoting cognitive achievements. *Elementary School Journal, 85,* 673–693.

Wixson, K. K., & Lipson, M. Y. (1991). *Reading diagnosis and remediation.* Glenview, IL: Scott, Foresman.

Motivation to Read Profile: Reading Survey

Name _____ **Date** _____

Sample 1: I am in _____.

☐ second grade   ☐ fifth grade

☐ third grade   ☐ sixth grade

☐ fourth grade

Sample 2: I am a _____.

☐ boy

☐ girl

1 My friends think I am _____.

☐ a very good reader

☐ a good reader

☐ an OK reader

☐ a poor reader

2 Reading a book is something I like to do _____.

☐ Never

☐ Not very often

☐ Sometimes

☐ Often

3 I read _____.

☐ not as well as my friends

☐ about the same as my friends

☐ a little better than my friends

☐ a lot better than my friends

4 My best friends think reading is _____.

☐ really fun

☐ fun

☐ OK to do

☐ no fun at all

(cont.)

5 When I come to a word I don't know, I can _____.

☐ almost always figure it out

☐ sometimes figure it out

☐ almost never figure it out

☐ never figure it out

6 I tell my friends about good books I read.

☐ I never do this.

☐ I almost never do this.

☐ I do this some of the time.

☐ I do this a lot.

7 When I am reading by myself, I understand _____.

☐ almost everything I read

☐ some of what I read

☐ almost none of what I read

☐ none of what I read

8 People who read a lot are _____.

☐ very interesting

☐ interesting

☐ not very interesting

☐ boring

9 I am _____.

☐ a poor reader

☐ an OK reader

☐ a good reader

☐ a very good reader

10 I think libraries are _____.

☐ a great place to spend time

☐ an interesting place to spend time

☐ an OK place to spend time

☐ a boring place to spend time

(cont.)

11 I worry about what other kids think about my reading _____.

☐ every day

☐ almost every day

☐ once in a while

☐ never

12 Knowing how to read well is _____.

☐ not very important

☐ sort of important

☐ important

☐ very important

13 When my teacher asks me a question about what I have read, I _____.

☐ can never think of an answer

☐ have trouble thinking of an answer

☐ sometimes think of an answer

☐ always think of an answer

14 I think reading is _____.

☐ a boring way to spend time

☐ an OK way to spend time

☐ an interesting way to spend time

☐ a great way to spend time

15 Reading is _____.

☐ very easy for me

☐ kind of easy for me

☐ kind of hard for me

☐ very hard for me

16 When I grow up I will spend _____.

☐ none of my time reading

☐ very little of my time reading

☐ some of my time reading

☐ a lot of my time reading

(cont.)

17 When I am in a group talking about stories, I _____.

☐ almost never talk about my ideas

☐ sometimes talk about my ideas

☐ almost always talk about my ideas

☐ always talk about my ideas

18 I would like for my teacher to read books out loud to the class _____.

☐ every day

☐ almost every day

☐ once in a while

☐ never

19 When I read out loud I am a _____.

☐ poor reader

☐ OK reader

☐ good reader

☐ very good reader

20 When someone gives me a book for a present, I feel _____.

☐ very happy

☐ sort of happy

☐ sort of unhappy

☐ unhappy

Motivation to Read Profile: Conversational Interview

Name _____ Date _____

A. Emphasis: Narrative Text

Suggested prompt (designed to engage the student in a natural conversation): I have been reading a good book . . . I was talking with . . . about it last night. I enjoy talking about good stories and books that I've been reading. Today I'd like to hear about what you have been reading.

1 Tell me about the most interesting story or book you have read this week (or even last week). Take a few minutes to think about it. (Wait time.) Now, tell me about the book or story.

Probes: What else can you tell me? Is there anything else?

_____

_____

_____

_____

_____

_____

_____

_____

2 How did you know or find out about this story? _____

_____

☐ assigned ☐ in school

☐ chosen ☐ out of school

3 Why was this story interesting to you? _____

_____

_____

_____

B. Emphasis: Informational Text

Suggested prompt (designed to engage student in a natural conversation): Often we read to find out about something or to learn about something. We read for information. For example, I remember a

(cont.)

Motivation to Read Profile: Conversational Interview *(cont.)*

student of mine . . . who read a lot of books about . . . to find out as much as he/she could about. . . . Now, I'd like to hear about some of the informational reading you have been doing.

1   Think about something important that you learned recently, not from your teacher and not from television, but from a book or some other reading material. What did you read about? (Wait time.) Tell me about what you learned.

Probes: What else could you tell me? Is there anything else?

_____

_____

_____

_____

_____

2   How did you know or find out about this book/article? _____

_____

_____

☐ assigned   ☐ in school

☐ chosen   ☐ out of school

3   Why was this book (or article) important to you? _____

_____

_____

_____

C. Emphasis: General Reading

1   Did you read anything at home yesterday? _____ What?

_____

_____

2   Do you have any books at school (in your desk/storage area/locker/book bag) today that you are reading? _____ Tell me about them.

_____

_____

_____

(cont.)

Motivation to Read Profile: Conversational Interview *(cont.)*

3 Tell me about your favorite author.

_____

_____

_____

4 What do you think you have to learn to be a better reader?

_____

_____

_____

5 Do you know about any books right now that you'd like to read? Tell me about them.

_____

_____

_____

6 How did you find out about these books?

_____

_____

_____

7 What are some things that get you really excited about reading books?

_____

_____

Tell me about . . .

_____

_____

_____

8 Who gets you really interested and excited about reading books?

_____

_____

Tell me more about what they do.

_____

_____

_____

FORM C

Motivation to Read Profile: Reading Survey Scoring Sheet

Student name _____

Grade _____ **Teacher** _____

Administration date _____

Recoding scale
1 = 4
2 = 3
3 = 2
4 = 1

Self-Concept as a Reader		Value of Reading	
*recode	1. _____		2. _____
	3. _____	*recode	4. _____
*recode	5. _____		6. _____
*recode	7. _____	*recode	8. _____
	9. _____	*recode	10. _____
	11. _____		12. _____
	13. _____		14. _____
*recode	15. _____		16. _____
	17. _____	*recode	18. _____
	19. _____	*recode	20. _____

SC raw score: _____/40   V raw score: _____/40

Full survey raw score (Self Concept & Value): _____/80

Percentage scores: Self-Concept   [   ]

                                  Value   [   ]

                          Full Survey   [   ]

Comments: _____

_____

_____

_____

_____

The Teacher, the Text, and the Context as Factors in Motivating Students to Write

The Motivation to Write Scale

Studies of the emergent literacy period reveal that when allowed and encouraged to explore literacy, young children learn about written language very naturally (Harste, Woodward, & Burke, 1984; Holdaway, 1979; Strickland & Morrow, 1989). In fact, young children often show an interest in writing before they actually read (Bissex, 1980; Durkin, 1966; Hall, Moretz, & Statom, 1976). Calkins (1986) contends that human beings have an innate need to write, which helps us to understand and organize our personal experiences.

Despite this seemingly natural inclination to write, teachers often encounter students who do not view writing as a meaningful or purposeful activity, or one in which they would engage by choice. Some children appear to be highly motivated to engage in writing while others will go to great lengths to avoid any task that involves writing. Calkins (1986) goes on to point out that many students will complete assigned writing tasks without ever becoming "deeply and personally involved in their writing" (p. 5).

Engaging students in writing and providing them with sustained opportunities to write is important for improving their writing abilities (Applebee, Langer, Mullis, Latham, & Gentile, 1994). This was one of several important findings that

This chapter is an adapted version of Codling, R. M., Gambrell, L. B., Kennedy, E., Palmer, B. M., & Graham, M. (1996). Reading Research Report No. 59. Reprinted by permission from the National Reading Research Center. The Data Analysis and Results sections of the original report have been excluded here. Readers interested in seeing the full text can find it online at *www.eric.ed.gov/PDFS/ ED398548.pdf.*

resulted from the most recent National Assessment of Educational Progress (NAEP) conducted among 4th-, 5th-, and 12th-grade students around the nation. A second finding was that many students find writing difficult and perform poorly on certain types of writing. Students found narrative writing tasks the least difficult while the majority of students produced only "minimally developed" responses to the informative writing tasks. Students at all three grade levels found persuasive writing the most difficult, especially the task of providing evidence to support their arguments. Additionally, students who reported enjoying writing had higher average writing proficiency than students who said they did not like to write.

Teachers are more interested than ever before in how to motivate children to write and how to help them become good, effective writers. The current interest in writing is largely a result of the knowledge that writing proficiency is a critical factor in educating students for the diverse demands of today's society (Freedman, Dyson, Flower, & Chafe, 1987; Graves, 1995).

What initiates and sustains students' motivation to write? How do teachers nurture and support students in their writing development? These questions guided the present investigation.

Motivation

Motivation has been studied from many perspectives in a number of different fields. From this body of work, we know that motivation is a fascinating and complex phenomenon in which various factors interact to produce different patterns of motivational behavior (Ford, 1992; McCombs, 1991; Oldfather, 1993). Two factors that have consistently emerged in past research on motivation are task value and self-perceived competence.

Expectancy–value theory posits that the value an individual places on a task or goal determines whether or not the individual will expend the effort necessary to accomplish it. For example, imagine an individual who learns that her company is expanding and will be opening a new branch office in 2 years. Having had 15 years of experience in the field and 10 years with the company, she feels that she would have a tremendous advantage for promotion. However, she also realizes that she will need to complete her college degree in order to qualify for a new position. Her decision to complete her schooling will be largely influenced by the value she affords to the new position. If she feels that acquiring the new job is personally valuable to her, she is likely to spend an inordinate amount of time doing whatever is necessary to reach that goal.

Other theories of motivation also attach importance to the construct of "value." In Ford's (1992) motivational systems theory, goals are most likely to be pursued if they are personally relevant and important. Self-determination theory posits that individuals will be more willing to engage in activities, even those that are not of inherent interest, if the ultimate goal is of personal value (Deci, Vallerand, Pelletier, & Ryan, 1991). In addition, research has shown that students who perceive a task as important will engage in the task in a more planful and effortful manner (Ames & Archer, 1988; Dweck & Elliott, 1983; Paris & Oka, 1986).

A second factor that influences an individual's motivation is self-perceived competence. An individual's sense of personal competence at achieving a goal directly influences that person's decision to pursue the goal. In the previous example, the worker who has fulfilled past job requirements efficiently is likely to have a sense that she can handle new responsibilities. In addition, if she has experienced success at school experiences in the past, she may be willing to take the classes necessary to complete her degree. Conversely, if she has had difficulty fulfilling her present job requirements, has been unsuccessful at schooling in the past, or for some other reason anticipates being unable to reach her goal because she lacks competence, she is not as likely to pursue the new position.

This example demonstrates how an individual's expectations of success or failure, based on his or her sense of personal competence, influence motivation. Many studies lend support to the important role of self-competence in task engagement (Bandura, 1989; Covington, 1985; Deci et al., 1991; Dweck, 1986; Spaulding, 1992; Weiner, 1990).

Because task value and self-perceived competence interact in important ways to influence motivation, they became the focal points for assessing students' levels of writing motivation in this study. A survey instrument that focuses on these two constructs was developed and used with students.

The Social Context of Learning and Motivation

Children come to understand written language in much the same way they learn spoken language. It is through interaction with other people engaged in the authentic uses of written language that meaning is constructed (Dyson, 1989).

Recent views of learning acknowledge the important role of social factors in the classroom learning environment (Hamilton, 1983). In fact, a number of social factors have been shown to mediate behavior, affect, and cognition. For example, Forman and Cazden (1994) demonstrated through an intensive set of investigations that peers working in either a tutoring or collaborative setting can accomplish cognitive tasks together that they could not accomplish alone. This extends the Vygotskian (1978) concept of scaffolding in which cognitive growth results from the interaction between a child and an adult. More importantly, it highlights the important role of peer interaction in the classroom setting.

A number of studies support the important role of social factors in motivation. Ames (1984) found that structural characteristics of school systems affect motivation. For instance, competitive environments encourage students to engage in social comparisons and their goal becomes one of trying to "look better" than other students. Within this context, ability is valued more than effort. A cooperative environment, in contrast, focuses on mastery of the task and learning as an end in itself. In this case, one competes only with oneself and effort becomes salient over ability.

Other investigations have also found that motivation is enhanced when the teacher provides an environment that encourages students to adopt a learning-oriented, rather than a performance-oriented, stance (Ames & Archer, 1988; Dweck, 1986; Nolen, 1988).

The Study

The present study explored children's motivation to write using a variety of data sources. Classroom observations, student surveys, student interviews, and teacher surveys revealed layers of detailed information on what motivates children to create meaning about written language within the social context of the classroom. The analysis of data from several sources enabled an integrative interpretation that provided a view of the lived experiences of these students (Moss, 1994).

Participants and Setting

The populations of the schools in which this study was conducted represent a range of ethnic and socioeconomic groups. Three schools and a total of 145 students participated. These students came from eight classrooms in the schools described below. Four of the classrooms were comprised of third graders ($N = 72$); four were comprised of fifth graders ($N = 73$).

School A is located in a community of approximately 186,000 people, just outside a large metropolitan city. The school has a student enrollment of 568. The ethnic majority is Hispanic (44%). Other nationalities represented include African American (34%), Caucasian (12%), and Asian (9%). Sixty-seven percent of the students qualify for the free/reduced-price lunch program.

School B is situated in a rapidly growing suburb of the same city, with a population just over 100,000. The school enrolls 565 students. Seventy-six percent of the students are Caucasian, 19% are African American, 2% are Asian, 2% are Hispanic, while less than 1% is Native American. The free/reduced-price lunch program is utilized by 17% of the students.

School C is located in a nearby community of approximately 60,000 people and is described by the principal as primarily a farming community. The school has an enrollment of 921. The majority of students are Caucasian (90%) followed in number by African American (6%). Free/reduced-price lunches are received by 3% of the students.

The experience of the eight participating teachers ranged from 1 year to 21 years, with a mean of 12 years of experience. The teachers in this study reported learning how to teach writing from undergraduate and graduate courses and from inservice sessions. Two teachers rated their writing instruction as satisfactory, four rated themselves as good, and two as excellent.

The eight teachers in this study reported using a variety of approaches to reading instruction. All of the teachers use children's literature or a combination of basal readers and children's literature. They reported involving their students in a variety of activities. For example, the children most often engage in brainstorming, creative writing, and revision. Many students also write in some type of journal. Teachers themselves appear to make use of mini-lessons, written feedback, holistic scoring, and teacher–student conferences.

Procedures and Materials

Data for this study were collected through classroom observations, student surveys, and student interviews. In addition, teacher surveys were administered. The study was conducted over a 4-month period. First, full-day observations were conducted in each of the target classrooms in November and December. These observations provided an overall sense of the literacy program that existed in each classroom. The observations also served to validate teacher and student reports about typical classroom activities. In early January, the students responded to a survey, the Motivation to Write Scale (MWS). The MWS is a two-part questionnaire designed to elicit information about students' self-perceived competence and the value they place on writing. Toward the end of January, 10 students were randomly selected from each classroom to participate in the Motivation to Write Interview. The interview provided personally relevant information about the writing of individual students. In early February, the teachers completed a written survey that tapped information about their backgrounds and typical writing instruction in their classrooms.

Motivation to Write Scale

Based on the important influence of task value and self-competence on motivation, the MWS was developed by the researchers to focus on these constructs (see Form D). Part I, "What Do *You* Think about Writing?" explores the value children place on writing. It includes 14 Likert-type items, each with four possible responses. In order to avoid repetition in the presentation of the response alternatives and to control for the threat of "response set" (i.e., children selecting the same response for each item), some response alternatives proceed from most to least positive while others are ordered in the opposite way. Items focus on issues that reflect the value students attach to writing tasks, such as writing narrative and informational text, sharing writing, and time spent writing. The last item in Part I of the MWS (#15) requests students to indicate which one of several options they would select if they were given a choice of writing activities. Students are directed to check *one* activity to show their preference.

Part II, "How Do You *Feel* about Your Writing?" examines students' self-concepts as writers. It contains 12 items designed to detect how students feel about their competence as authors of expository and narrative text. This scale also includes Likert-type items, and the four response options again alternate from positive to negative or negative to positive. The last item in Part II (#13) taps information about the writing activities students engage in on a regular basis. This item requests students to indicate the kinds of writing they have done *this week.*

The two parts of the MWS were administered to 72 third-grade and 73 fifth-grade students in their own classrooms. They were administered by research assistants on different days during the same week. Students were given directions to listen as the items were read aloud by the research assistant and then mark their answers. The MWS items were read aloud to remove reading ability as a possible confounding variable.

Motivation to Write Interview

An interview was developed by the researchers for use in this study (see Form E). Researchers have a long-standing tradition of using interviews to gather information about the experiences of others (Fontana & Frey, 1994). Listening to the perspectives of research subjects reveals important insights for understanding their world (Seidman, 1991). In order to capture the essence of students' opinions and experiences, the semistructured interview used in this study utilized open-ended questions (Goetz & LeCompte, 1984; Silverman, 1993). However, the questions were used flexibly and interesting leads were explored by the interviewer.

The interview questions were primarily open-ended and children were encouraged to elaborate with prompts such as "Tell me about that" and "Can you tell me any more?". Prior to general use, the interview was pilot-tested to clarify the wording of questions and estimate time requirements.

Interview questions focus on five areas of interest with regard to writing. First, we were interested in learning about specific writing experiences of the students. Students recalled and described a specific piece of writing they had recently completed. Second, we inquired about the more general writing experiences students had. We asked questions such as "Do you ever talk to anyone at home about the things you write?" A third area of interest was the connection students made between their past and present literacy experiences, a concept called "intertextuality" (Cairney, 1990). We asked, "Do you ever think of stories you've read when you are writing a story?" Fourth, we asked questions about planning, drafting, and revising in order to acquire information on students' engagement in the writing process. Finally, we focused on the students' perceptions of their own writing competence. Forty students at each grade level were randomly selected to participate in the interviews. The students were interviewed individually for approximately 30 minutes, in a quiet area away from the classroom to avoid distractions. The interviews were tape-recorded and transcribed for later analysis. In order to determine patterns of response, a rubric was developed that quantified much of the information provided by students (see Form F). Two research assistants read through 10% of the transcribed interviews at each grade level and scored the student responses according to the rubric. When results were compared, interrater agreement was .94 for third grade and .95 for fifth grade. Responses on the remaining interviews were then analyzed according to the rubric.

Teacher Survey

At the conclusion of the data collection period, teachers were asked to respond to a survey that was designed to provide information about their backgrounds and writing instruction in their classrooms. Responses to the survey were then compared with the writing instruction that was observed.

The two-page survey contained general questions about grade level, teaching experience, training in writing instruction, and practices related to writing. The teachers were also asked to indicate the frequency with which they utilize certain student and teacher activities such as journal writing, revision, and mini-lessons.

Discussion

This study, while beginning to provide evidence about writing motivation, supports prior research on general motivation. That is, children's motivation to write is a complex issue, affected by many factors. For example, the teacher's attitude and actions, the type of text students read and write, and the context in which writing occurs are all factors that may have an impact on a child's motivation to write.

It is well established that in order to be motivated to engage in any activity, an individual must feel competent at accomplishing it. The teacher is in a position to provide the instruction support and scaffolding that is essential to move young writers forward in their development, thereby ensuring their competence.

Perhaps even more important may be the teacher's attitude toward writing. Teachers who believe writing to be important and interesting, and convey that attitude, encourage students to value writing as a worthwhile task.

The text students encounter in their reading has a strong influence on their writing. When children are exposed to a wide variety of reading materials, they are provided with sources for their own writing. Experience with high-quality, engaging expository text early in the school years may be an important vehicle for improving children's negative feelings related to writing information text.

Creating a motivating context for student writing is an important and challenging task for teachers. This study indicates that an important component of this kind of environment is social interaction. Children frequently commented that they share their writing with, and get ideas for writing from, friends, family members, and the teacher. Of particular interest was that students' perceptions of their own writing competence was often a reflection of how others reacted to their writing, suggesting that giving and receiving feedback should not be taken lightly. Rather, it should be carefully discussed and receive attention from an instructional standpoint.

The students in this study expressed a high level of interest when they were allowed to write about self-chosen topics. Other recent research also supports the notion that choice manifests control, which is an essential ingredient in intrinsic motivation (Deci et al., 1991; Turner & Paris, 1995). Creating a context in which children will be motivated means providing them with choices and opportunities to write for sustained periods of time.

Cooper (1993) maintains that motivation involves a complex set of ongoing activities and attitudes that occur in the classroom environment. These activities and attitudes help to build a community of learners who are excited about reading and writing and want to learn. The results of this study demonstrate that within these classroom communities, writing knowledge was socially constructed, and self-perceptions of writing ability were socially constructed as well. For these students, knowledge of writing was socially constructed through peer revision, comments during sharing, teacher editing and feedback, and certain types of instruction. Self-perceptions of writing ability appeared to be socially constructed through successful experiences, comments of others, and knowledge itself. The finding that social interaction played such a critical role in knowledge acquisition and self-perception of writing ability was an important one in this study. This study demonstrated that children come to value writing and to feel good about themselves as writers when they are given opportunities to engage in various kinds of writing in an environment in which social interaction is encouraged and instructional support is provided.

References

Ames, C. (1984). Competitive, cooperative, and individualized goal structures: A cognitive-motivational analysis. In R. E. Ames & C. Ames (Eds.), *Motivation in education* (Vol. 1, pp. 177–207). San Francisco: Academic Press.

Ames, C., & Archer, J. (1988). Achievement goals in the classroom: Students' learning strategies and motivation processes. *Journal of Educational Psychology, 80,* 260–267.

Applebee, A. N., Langer, J. A., Mullis, I. V. S., Latham, A. S., & Gentile, C. A. (1994). *NAEP 1992 writing report card.* Washington, DC: Office of Educational Research and Improvement.

Bandura, A. (1989). Human agency in social cognitive theory. *American Psychologist, 44,* 1175–1184.

Bissex, G. L. (1980). *Gnys at wrk: A child learns to write and read.* Cambridge, MA: Harvard University Press.

Cairney, T. (1990). Intertextuality: Infectious echoes from the past. *The Reading Teacher, 43,* 478–484.

Calkins, L. (1986). *The art of teaching writing.* Portsmouth, NH: Heinemann.

Cooper, J. D. (1993). *Literacy: Helping children construct meaning* (2nd ed.). Boston: Houghton Mifflin.

Covington, M. V. (1985). The motive for selfworth. In C. Ames & R. Ames (Eds.), *Research on motivation in education: The classroom milieu* (pp. 77–113). New York: Academic Press.

Deci, E. L., Vallerand, R. J., Pelletier, L. G., & Ryan, R. M. (1991). Motivation and education: The self-determination perspective. *Educational Psychologist, 26,* 325–346.

Durkin, D. (1966). *Children who read early.* New York: Teachers College Press.

Dweck, C. S. (1986). Motivational processes affecting learning. *American Psychologist, 41,* 1040–1048.

Dweck, C. S., & Elliott, E. (1983). Achievement motivation. In E. M. Heatherington (Ed.), *Handbook of child psychology: Vol. 4. Socialization, personality, and social development* (pp. 643–691). New York: Wiley.

Dyson, A. H. (1989). *Multiple worlds of child writers*. New York: Teachers College Press.

Fontana, A., & Frey, J. H. (1994). Interviewing: The art of science. In N. K. Denzin & Y. S. Lincoln (Eds.), *Handbook of qualitative research* (pp. 361–376). Thousand Oaks, CA: Sage.

Ford, M. E. (1992). *Motivating humans*. Newbury Park, CA: Sage.

Forman, E. A., & Cazden, C. B. (1994). Exploring Vygotskian perspectives in education: The cognitive value of peer interaction. In R. B. Ruddell, M. R. Ruddell, & H. Singer (Eds.), *Theoretical models and processes of reading* (4th ed., pp. 155–178). Newark, DE: International Reading Association.

Freedman, S. W., Dyson, A. H., Flower, L., & Chafe, W. (1987). *Research in writing: Past, present, and future* (Technical Report No. 1). Berkeley, CA: Center for the Study of Writing.

Goetz, J. P., & LeCompte, M. D. (1984). *Ethnography and qualitative design in educational research*. New York: Academic Press.

Graves, D. H. (1995). *A fresh look at writing*. Portsmouth, NH: Heinemann.

Hall, M. A., Moretz, S. A., & Statom, J. (1976). Writing before grade one: A study of early writers. *Language Arts, 53,* 582–585.

Hamilton, S. F. (1983). The social side of schooling: Ecological studies of classrooms and schools. *Elementary School Journal, 83,* 313–334.

Harste, J., Woodward, V., & Burke, C. (1984). *Language stories and literacy lessons*. Portsmouth, NH: Heinemann.

Holdaway, D. (1979). *The foundations of literacy*. New York: Ashton Scholastic.

McCombs, B. L. (1991). Unraveling motivation: New perspectives from research and practice. *Journal of Experimental Education, 60,* 3–88.

Moss, P. A. (1994). Can there be validity without reliability? *Educational Researcher, 23*(2), 5–12.

Nolen, S. B. (1988). Reasons for studying: Motivational orientations and study strategies. *Cognition and Instruction, 5,* 269–287.

Oldfather, P. (1993). What students say about motivating experiences in a whole language classroom. *The Reading Teacher, 46,* 672–681.

Paris, S. G., & Oka, E. R. (1986). Self-regulated learning among exceptional children. *Exceptional Children, 53,* 103–108.

Seidman, I. (1991). *Interviewing as qualitative research*. New York: Teachers College Press.

Silverman, D. (1993). *Interpreting qualitative data: Methods for analyzing talk, text, and interaction*. Thousand Oaks, CA: Sage.

Spaulding, C. L. (1992). The motivation to read and write. In J. W. Irwin & M. A. Doyle (Eds.), *Reading/writing connections: Learning from research* (pp. 177–201). Newark, DE: International Reading Association.

Strauss, A., & Corbin, J. (1990). *Basics of qualitative research*. Newbury Park, CA: Sage.

Strickland, D. S., & Morrow, L. M. (1989). *Emerging literacy: Young children learn to read and write*. Newark, DE: International Reading Association.

Turner, J., & Paris, S. G. (1995). How literacy tasks influence children's motivation for literacy. *The Reading Teacher, 48,* 662–673.

Vygotsky, L. S. (1978). *Mind in society: The development of higher psychological processes*. Cambridge, MA: Harvard University Press.

Weiner, B. (1990). History of motivational research in education. *Journal of Educational Psychology, 82,* 616–622.

FORM D

Motivation to Write Scale

Name _____

PART I. VALUE OF WRITING

What Do *You* Think about Writing?

Sample 1: I am in _____
- ☐ third grade
- ☐ fifth grade

Sample 2: I am a _____
- ☐ boy
- ☐ girl

1 I would like for my teacher to let us write STORIES _____.
- ☐ every day
- ☐ almost every day
- ☐ once in a while
- ☐ never

2 I would like for my teacher to let us write REPORTS _____.
- ☐ every day
- ☐ almost every day
- ☐ once in a while
- ☐ never

3 I share what I write with my classmates.
- ☐ I never do this.
- ☐ I almost never do this.
- ☐ I do this some of the time.
- ☐ I do this a lot.

(cont.)

Motivation to Write Scale *(cont.)*

4 Writing STORIES is something I like to do _____.

☐ often

☐ sometimes

☐ not very often

☐ never

5 Writing REPORTS is something I like to do _____.

☐ often

☐ sometimes

☐ not very often

☐ never

6 Knowing how to write well is _____.

☐ not important

☐ kind of important

☐ important

☐ very important

7 People who write a lot are _____.

☐ very interesting

☐ interesting

☐ not very interesting

☐ boring

8 I share what I write with my family.

☐ I never do this.

☐ I almost never do this.

☐ I do this some of the time.

☐ I do this a lot.

9 Other people in my house _____.

☐ spend a lot of time writing

☐ spend some of the time writing

☐ almost never write

☐ never write

(cont.)

10 When I grow up I think I will spend _____.

☐ none of my time writing

☐ very little of my time writing

☐ some of my time writing

☐ a lot of my time writing

11 I save the things I write.

☐ always

☐ usually

☐ sometimes

☐ never

12 I think writing STORIES is _____.

☐ a boring way to spend time

☐ an OK way to spend time

☐ an interesting way to spend time

☐ a great way to spend time

13 I think writing REPORTS is _____.

☐ a boring way to spend time

☐ an OK way to spend time

☐ an interesting way to spend time

☐ a great way to spend time

14 I write something _____.

☐ everyday

☐ almost every day

☐ once in a while

☐ hardly ever

15 If your teacher said that you could choose to do one of the following in the next 20 minutes, which *one* would you choose? Check only *one* thing below.

_____ Write a letter   _____ Write a poem   _____ Write a list

_____ Write in my journal   _____ Write a message or a note   _____ Write in my diary

_____ Write a story   _____ Write a report   _____ Write a paragraph

_____ Write a play   _____ Write study notes

(cont.)

Motivation to Write Scale *(cont.)*

PART II: SELF-CONCEPT AS A WRITER

How Do *You* Feel about Your Writing?

Sample 1: I am in _____.

☐ third grade

☐ fifth grade

Sample 2: I am a _____.

☐ boy

☐ girl

1 My friends think I am _____.

☐ a very good writer

☐ a good writer

☐ an OK writer

☐ a poor writer

2 When I write STORIES, I feel _____.

☐ very pleased about what I write

☐ pleased about what I write

☐ OK about what I write

☐ unhappy about what I write

3 When I write REPORTS, I feel _____.

☐ very pleased about what I write

☐ pleased about what I write

☐ OK about what I write

☐ unhappy about what I write

4 I like to read what I write to others.

☐ almost never

☐ sometimes

☐ almost always

☐ always

(cont.)

Motivation to Write Scale *(cont.)*

5 When I write STORIES, I think I am _____.

☐ a poor author

☐ an OK author

☐ a good author

☐ a very good author

6 When I write REPORTS, I think I am _____.

☐ a poor author

☐ an OK author

☐ a good author

☐ a very good author

7 When I don't know what to write about, I _____.

☐ almost always get an idea on my own

☐ sometimes get an idea on my own

☐ almost never get an idea on my own

☐ never get an idea on my own

8 The STORIES I write are usually _____.

☐ very good

☐ good

☐ OK

☐ poor

9 The REPORTS I write are usually _____.

☐ very interesting

☐ interesting

☐ OK

☐ boring

10 What others think about my writing is important to me _____.

☐ always

☐ almost always

☐ sometimes

☐ almost never

(cont.)

Motivation to Write Scale *(cont.)*

11 Writing STORIES is _____.

☐ very easy for me

☐ kind of easy for me

☐ kind of hard for me

☐ very hard for me

12 Writing REPORTS is _____.

☐ very easy for me

☐ kind of easy for me

☐ kind of hard for me

☐ very hard for me

13 Check *all* the items below that *you did this week.*

_____ 1. Wrote a story

_____ 2. Wrote a report

_____ 3. Wrote a play

_____ 4. Wrote notes

_____ 5. Wrote a poem

_____ 6. Wrote a message

_____ 7. Wrote a letter

_____ 8. Wrote a list

_____ 9. Wrote for fun

_____ 10. Wrote in my journal or diary

Motivation to Write: Student Interview

Specific Writing Experience

I'd like to talk about something you've written recently. Can you tell me about something you've written recently?

_____

_____

_____

What was it?

Why did you write it?

Where did you get your idea for this story?

Why did you choose to tell me about this?

Did you share your writing with anyone? Tell me about it.

Did you write this on a computer? _____ Yes _____ No

If No:

Do you ever write stories or reports on a computer? _____ Yes _____ No

Where is the computer? _____

Do you go to the computer lab at school? _____ Why/Why not?

_____

Do you own a computer? _____

Tell me about something that you've written recently that you thought wasn't very good.

What makes you say that it's not very good?

_____

_____

General Writing Experiences

Did you write anything at home yesterday? Tell me about it. Why did you write it?

If No: Do you ever write anything at home?

_____

Do you ever talk to anyone at home about what you write? Tell me about that.

_____

(cont.)

Motivation to Write: Student Interview *(cont.)*

Do you ever talk to anyone at school about what you write? Tell me about that.

_____

Do your classmates ever tell you how to improve your writing? How do you feel about that?
◆ Do they give you suggestions?
◆ What kind of suggestions do they give you?
◆ Do you have a particular friend or group of friends that you share your writing with?

_____

_____

Why do you think people write? What are important reasons for writing?

_____

Who gets you interested and excited about writing? Tell me about it.

_____

◆ Is there anything else that gets you excited about writing? _____

Have you ever felt really good about something that you've written? _____
◆ What was it?
◆ Tell me why you felt good about it.

_____

_____

Do you have any writing plans right now . . . something you've been thinking about writing?
If No: When will you write again?

_____

Intertextuality

Do you ever think of stories you've read when you are writing a story? _____ Yes _____ No
If Yes:
◆ Give me an example.
◆ What was the name of the story you thought about?
◆ How was your story like the story you read?
◆ How was your story different from the story you read?

_____

_____

Is there anything else that you can think of that gives you ideas for writing?

_____

(cont.)

Motivation to Write: Student Interview *(cont.)*

Writing Process

Do you think about what you are going to write *before* you write it? Tell me about it.

Do you do anything in particular? Tell me about it.

_____

Do you revise your writing and sometimes make changes? _____

- ◆ Tell me about something you wrote that you revised or changed.
- ◆ What were some of the changes you made?
- ◆ Why did you revise it?

_____

_____

Writer Competence

What kind of writer do you think you are? (*Show cards:* Terrific   Good   Fair   Crummy)

- ◆ Why do you think you are a _____ writer?

_____

What do you think you have to learn to be a better writer?

- ◆ Anything else that you think would make you a better writer?

_____

What do you think makes someone a good writer?

_____

What does your teacher do that helps you to be a good writer?

_____

How does your teacher decide which students are good writers?

_____

Does your teacher grade your writing? (*Ask for details.*)

_____

Does your teacher sit down and talk with you about your writing? Tell me about that.

_____

Does your teacher ever teach lessons about how to be a better writer? Tell me about that.

- ◆ Can you give me an example?

_____

FORM F

Scoring Rubric for Motivation to Write Interviews

	Subjects		
Writing Experiences			
Specific titles of original writing			
Elaborated information on original writing			
Vague description of original writing			
Chosen			
Assigned			
Sharing of original work			
with teacher			
with classmates/friends			
with family			
Participation in Writer's Workshop			
Type of writing they chose to tell about			
story			
letter			
poem			
informational			
Where did you get your idea? (for writing)			
curriculum content			
TV			
book			

(cont.)

From Codling, Gambrell, Kennedy, Palmer, and Graham (1996). Reprinted by ptermission from the National Reading Research Center in *Maximizing Motivation for Literacy Learning: Grades K–6* by Barbara A. Marinak, Linda B. Gambrell, and Susan A. Mazzoni (Guilford Press, 2013). Permission to photocopy this form is granted to purchasers of this book for personal use only (see copyright page for details).

Scoring Rubric for Motivation to Write Interviews *(cont.)*

Why choose to tell me about this?			
most recent			
best work			
Computer			
lab in school			
attend lab once/week			
attend lab more than once/week			
own a computer			
enjoy using a computer			
reasons for using the computer			
it's fun			
games			
writing			
drawing			
math			
Tell about writing that wasn't good			
Why writing wasn't good			
too few details included (information)			
not enough descriptive language			
length			
Write at home yesterday?			
Ever write at home?			

(cont.)

Scoring Rubric for Motivation to Write Interviews *(cont.)*

Kind of writing done at home			
homework			
stories			
journal			
Talk with anyone about writing?			
parents			
siblings			
teacher			
classmates/friends			
Classmates give ideas to improve writing?			
handwriting (penmanship)			
mechanics (grammar/punctuation/capitalization)			
making sense			
elaborating			
use the dictionary			
sentence-related			
word-related			
Why do people write?			
express themselves/communicate			
to learn			
future-/job-related			
for fun			
to improve writing skills			

(cont.)

Scoring Rubric for Motivation to Write Interviews *(cont.)*

Who/what gets you interested in writing? _____			
parents _____			
siblings _____			
teacher _____			
classmates/friends _____			
_____			
_____			
sports _____			
TV _____			
movies _____			
_____			
Ever felt very good about something written? _____			
specific title of original writing _____			
elaborated description _____			
vague description of original writing _____			
Why did you feel good about it? _____			
simply describes story _____			
people wanted to read it _____			
best work _____			
_____			
_____			
Do you have writing plans now? _____			
Specific plans (topic/title/plot/idea) _____			

Intertextuality

Do you ever think of stories you read when you are writing a story? _____			
books _____			
classmates' stories _____			
siblings _____			
teacher _____			

(cont.)

Scoring Rubric for Motivation to Write Interviews *(cont.)*

drawing _____			
content journals/notebooks/learning logs _____			
_____			
_____			

Writing Process

Plan your writing? _____			
Revise writing? _____			
Why revise? _____			
make it better _____			
make it more interesting _____			
check spelling _____			
make it sensible _____			

Writer Competence

What kind of writer are you?			
terrific _____			
good _____			
fair _____			
poor _____			
Why?			
think of ideas easily _____			
make too many mistakes _____			
don't finish stories _____			
stories are too short _____			
stories don't make sense _____			
How can you become a better writer?			
spell better _____			
type better _____			
improve handwriting _____			
work beyond initial draft _____			

(cont.)

Scoring Rubric for Motivation to Write Interviews *(cont.)*

learn to make it more interesting			
make it more sensible			
read more			
write more			

What makes someone a good writer?

imagination			
good ideas			
good spelling			
someone who reads/likes to read			
someone who writes/likes to write			
instruction			

Teacher Influence

What does the teacher do to help you become a better writer?

conferences			
edits			
offers suggestions			
add details			
word-related			
sentence-/paragraph-related			
ideas to write about			
says "write more"			
reads aloud			

(cont.)

teaches strategies			
Teacher grade stories?			
Teacher grade other writing?			
letter grades			
comments			
Teacher teach lessons on becoming a better writer?			
Directed Oral Language (DOL)			
capitalization/punctuation			

FORM G

Honor All Print Survey

1 What kind of texts do you like to read?

☐ Fiction

☐ Graphic novels

☐ Comic books

☐ Fact/list books

☐ Jokes/riddles

☐ Nonfiction

☐ Poetry

☐ Newspapers

☐ Magazines

☐ Articles on the Internet

2 If you like to read fiction, what kind of fiction do you like to read?

☐ Realistic

☐ Folktales

☐ Fantasy

☐ Mystery

☐ Historical fiction

☐ Science fiction

☐ Survival

3 If you like to read graphic novels, what kind of graphic novels do you like to read?

_____

_____

_____

4 If you like to read comic books, what are a few of your favorites?

_____

_____

_____

(cont.)

Honor All Print Survey *(cont.)*

5 If you like to read fact/list books, what are a few of your favorites?

_____

_____

_____

6 If you like to read nonfiction books, what topics do you like to read about?

_____

_____

_____

7 If you like to read newspapers, what sections do you like to read?

_____

_____

_____

8 If you like to read magazines, what are a few of your favorites?

_____

_____

_____

9 If you like to read articles on the Internet, what are a few of your favorite websites?

_____

_____

_____

10 What other texts do you like to read?

_____

_____

_____

PART SIX

Conclusion
Myths and Truths Revisited

The Myths and Truths Survey presented at the beginning of this book was designed to promote reflection prior to considering the motivating techniques presented in the first three parts: *Motivating Classroom Communities, Promoting Self-Concept as a Reader,* and *Promoting the Value of Reading.* As mentioned in the introduction to the survey, the items were collected from teachers and teacher educators when they were asked two questions: What are *myths* related to nurturing intrinsic reading motivation? What are *truths* related to nurturing intrinsic reading motivation? As you noticed on the response options, a statement could be a *myth*, a *truth*, or a *depends. Depends* is a critical option on such a survey because many aspects of nurturing intrinsic motivation depend on the conditions and context in which the action is carried out.

We hope the survey provided a framework for you and your colleagues to begin thinking about *myths* and *truths* related to intrinsic motivation. Perhaps it also promoted conversation in your professional learning community. Now, in light of evidence-based practices related to nurturing reading motivation, we conclude with our perspectives on the items in the Myths and Truths Survey (see Figure 1).

1 **Teachers are critical to nurturing and maintaining reading motivation.** This statement is true. *You* are critical to nurturing and maintaining reading motivation in your classroom. Research indicates that the kind of literacy community you nurture in your classroom can serve to either support or undermine intrinsic reading motivation (Allington & Johnston, 2002; Pressley, Allington, Wharton-McDonald, Block, & Morrow, 2001). Providing a community that is print-rich, honors all types of reading, and provides students with literacy choices are a few of the important

1. Teachers are critical to nurturing and maintaining reading motivation.	M Ⓣ D
2. Public displays of achievement undermine intrinsic reading motivation.	M Ⓣ D
3. Providing choice nurtures intrinsic reading motivation.	M Ⓣ D
4. Tasks and text within the zone of proximal development are motivating.	M Ⓣ D
5. Boys are less motivated to read than girls.	M T Ⓓ
6. Extrinsic rewards always lead to intrinsic motivation.	Ⓜ T D
7. Teacher read-alouds are motivating.	M T Ⓓ
8. Struggling readers are generally less motivated to read than proficient readers.	M Ⓣ D
9. Motivation declines as grade levels increase.	M Ⓣ D
10. All students lack the motivation to read complex text.	Ⓜ T D
11. Girls like to read fiction; boys like to read nonfiction.	Ⓜ T D
12. Motivation is an important scaffold when text becomes challenging.	M Ⓣ D
13. Teachers cannot impact the motivation to read.	Ⓜ T D
14. Authentic reading experiences are motivating.	M Ⓣ D
15. Motivation is idiosyncratic.	M Ⓣ D

FIGURE 1. Myths and Truths Survey: Our responses. *Response codes:* M, myth; T, truth; D, depends.

motivation practices you control. We hope the methods in this book have offered easy-to-implement ideas for nurturing intrinsic reading motivation in your classroom community.

2 **Public displays of reading achievement undermine intrinsic motivation.** This statement is also true. Reading achievement is highly variable in any classroom and public displays of such differences can undermine the self-confidence of some readers, particularly those who struggle with literacy learning. In addition, such displays can erode trust in the literacy community. At a time when readers must take risks to learn, public displays of achievement discourage the collaboration necessary for all students to reach their maximum potential (Cunningham & Allington, 2007).

3 **Providing choice nurtures intrinsic reading motivation.** No doubt about it, choice is motivating. Research suggests that choice is a powerful force that allows students to take ownership and responsibility for their learning (Rettig & Hendricks, 2000). Studies also indicate that motivation increases when students have opportunities to make choices about what they learn and when they believe they have some autonomy or control over their own learning (Jang, Reeve, & Deci, 2010; Skinner & Belmont, 1993). Recognizing that flexibility is sometimes hard to find in this era of high-stakes accountability, we hope this book offers a variety of ways to provide student choice without compromising the integrity of your curricular expectations.

4 **Tasks and texts within the zone of proximal development are motivating.** Theory and research supports the conclusion that tasks and texts offered within the zone of proximal development are motivating (Edmonds et al., 2009; Vygotsky, 1978). Having said that, however, it is important to continually monitor the zone. As children grow in their reading proficiency, release responsibility back to them. As Clay (1998) reminds us, texts and tasks should always provide "sufficient challenge." Rigor is motivating!

5 **Boys are less motivated to read than girls.** This is a tricky statement. It depends. It has been known for a number of years that adolescent boys report lower motivation to read than adolescent girls. However, recent investigations reveal that gender differences related to motivation are present even in young readers (Merisuo-Storm, 2006; Mohr, 2006; Pappas, 1993). In one of our studies, we found that the motivation of boys begins to erode as early as second grade (Marinak & Gambrell, 2010). The good news is that in that same study boys told us during Conversational Interviews of the Motivation to Read Profile (Gambrell, Palmer, Codling, & Mazzoni, 1996) how to prevent their motivation from eroding. Much of what they described can be found in this book's methods, including more choices, access to a wide variety of print, and authentic tasks. Several of the methods were put to the test during a fifth-grade research study. You can read about our findings in this investigation in the case study in Part Four.

6 **Extrinsic rewards always lead to intrinsic motivation.** Research suggests that this statement is a myth (Cameron & Pierce, 1994; Deci, 1971, 1972). In fact, under many conditions, extrinsic rewards actually undermine intrinsic motivation. Therefore, it appears that if extrinsic reading rewards are used, we need to carefully consider the type of reward and conditions under which the reward is offered. An example from our research might help illustrate this point (Marinak & Gambrell, 2008). We found that the use of proximal rewards (giving a book for reading) did not undermine intrinsic reading motivation when compared to rewards less proximal to reading (e.g., Nerf balls, Pez dispensers). Therefore, when extrinsic rewards are offered, they should be a natural extension of a literacy-rich classroom culture. In addition, there are numerous "rewarding" methods in this book that can be used as a natural extension of a literacy-rich culture, including *Your Life in Books, Honor All Print*, and *Now–Next–Quick Reads*, to name just a few.

7 **Teacher read-alouds are motivating.** This is a tough one. As much as we want to believe that teacher read-alouds are always motivating for our students, it appears that this is not always true. Our research indicates that boys are especially sensitive to the teacher read-aloud (Marinak & Gambrell, 2009). In interviews with elementary students, boys often indicated they did not enjoy the teacher's read-aloud because "the teacher reads too many girl books" or "they don't read the kind of books I like." Knowing that teacher read-alouds grow vocabulary, we suggest using *Vote for the Read-Aloud* to invite reluctant listeners into this important experience.

8 **Struggling readers are generally less motivated to read than proficient readers.** It should be no surprise to classroom teachers that this statement is true. It is not easy to be a struggling reader. Numerous studies have documented the finding that struggling elementary readers report lower reading motivation than their more proficient peers (Allington, 2006; Anderson & Pellicier, 1990). The methods in this book were carefully designed to nurture intrinsic motivation in all readers regardless of achievement. In other words, while your struggling readers are receiving instruction and intervention to grow their proficiency, try using our suggestions simultaneously to support reading motivation.

9 **Motivation declines as grade levels increase.** Research does indicate that motivation declines as grade levels increase, especially for boys (McKenna, Kear, & Ellsworth, 1995). In light of these findings, it is important to regularly assess reading interests and motivation, taking action as soon as you suspect motivation is eroding. *Maximizing Motivation* contains several assessment tools to help. The Motivation to Read Profile and the Honor All Print Survey are included in Part Five for your use. As an assessment extension, the Motivation to Write Scale is also provided.

10 **All students lack the motivation to read complex text.** This statement is also a myth. Rigor is very motivating for many students (Teale & Gambrell, 2007; Taylor, Pearson, Peterson, & Rodriguez, 2003). The key to maintaining intrinsic reading motivation when text becomes complex is teacher scaffolding. Challenging material can be motivating for students when the text is authentic and relevant, and when students are provided with a clear purpose for reading.

11 **Girls like to read fiction, boys like to read nonfiction.** Though a long-standing belief, recent research indicates that it is a myth. Both girls and boys appear very motivated to read informational text, even in the primary grades (Merisuo-Storm, 2006; Mohr, 2006; Pappas, 1993). And though informational text is sometimes challenging to comprehend, the more experience readers have with this genre, the more effective and motivated they will become.

12 **Motivation is an important scaffold when text becomes challenging.** As Gambrell (1996) noted, "Motivation makes the difference between learning that is superficial and shallow and learning that is deep and internalized" (p. 15). In other words, it is motivation that causes readers to risk and persist when text becomes challenging. This truth is important to bear in mind as all children face increasingly more rigorous literacy demands.

13 **Teachers cannot impact students' motivation to read.** Several decades of research clearly indicates that this is a myth (Brophy, 2008; Jang et al., 2010). Teachers are critical in the literacy lives of young readers. This is true as students become skillful and strategic. But it is also true as they develop (or not) intrinsic motivation. The case study in Part Four is an example of how small changes in practice can result in big motivational differences.

14 **Authentic reading experiences are motivating.** Authenticity is very motivating. Studies indicate that reading authentic texts for real purposes supports intrinsic reading motivation more so than engaging in literacy tasks over which students have little or no control (Brophy, 1998; Gambrell, Hughes, Calvert, Malloy, & Igo, 2011; Turner & Paris, 1995).

15 **Motivation is idiosyncratic.** We saved arguably the most important concept of the Myths and Truths Survey for last. Though motivation trends can be gleaned from research, the reality of being human is that motivation is idiosyncratic. It is highly individualized and nested in the social interactions of school, home, and community (Brophy, 2008; Guthrie & Cox, 2001). Consequently, in order to truly nurture and sustain intrinsic motivation, we must arrange reading tasks that lie within what Jere Brophy called the "motivational zone of proximal development" (1999, p. 77). These experiences are an optimal match for students in terms of both strategic challenge and personal interest. One method that celebrates the idiosyncratic nature of reading motivation is *Personal Invitation to Read*. It is when we connect with students about their individual text interests that reading becomes a rewarding experience.

Closing Thoughts

In his book *Catching Up or Leading the Way: American Education in the Age of Globalization*, Yong Zhao (2009) discusses the importance of intrinsic motivation in school and in life. He notes that when people (leaders, teachers, learners, etc.) are intrinsically motivated, they will become courageous. We hope the methods in *Maximizing Motivation* invite your young readers into courageous, intrinsically motivated reading.

References

Allington, R. L. (2006). *What really matters for struggling readers: Designing research-based programs* (2nd ed.). Boston: Pearson/Allyn & Bacon.

Allington, R. L., & Johnston, P. H. (2002). *Reading to learn: Lessons from exemplary fourth-grade classrooms.* New York: Guilford Press.

Anderson, L. W., & Pellicier, L. O. (1990). Synthesis of research on compensatory and remedial education. *Educational Leadership, 48*(1), 10–16.

Brophy, J. (1998). *Motivating students to learn.* Boston: McGraw-Hill.

Brophy, J. (1999). Toward a model of the value aspects of motivation in education: Developing appreciation for particular learning domains and activities. *Educational Psychologist, 34*(2), 75–85.

Brophy, J. (2008). Developing students' appreciation for what is taught in school. *Educational Psychologist, 43*(3), 132–141.

Cameron, J., & Pierce, W. D. (1994). Reinforcement, reward, and intrinsic motivation: A meta-analysis. *Review of Educational Research, 64*, 363–424.

Clay, M. (1998). *By different paths to common outcomes*. New York: Stenhouse.

Cunningham, P. M., & Allington, R. L. (2007). *Classrooms that work: They can all read and write* (3rd ed.). Boston: Allyn & Bacon.

Deci, E. L. (1971). Effects of externally mediated rewards on intrinsic motivation. *Journal of Personality and Social Psychology, 18*, 105–115.

Deci, E. L. (1972). Intrinsic motivation, extrinsic reinforcement, and inequity. *Journal of Personality and Social Psychology, 22*, 113–120.

Edmonds, M. S., Vaughn, S., Wexler, J., Reutebuch, C., Cable, A., Tacett, K. K., et al. (2009). A synthesis of reading interventions and effects on reading comprehension outcomes for older struggling readers. *Review of Educational Research, 79*(1), 262–300.

Gambrell, L. B. (1996). Creating classroom cultures that foster reading motivation. *The Reading Teacher, 50*(1), 14–25.

Gambrell, L. B., Hughes, E., Calvert, W., Malloy, J., & Igo, B. (2011). Authentic reading, writing, and discussion: An exploratory study of a pen pal project. *Elementary School Journal, 112*(2), 234–258.

Gambrell, L., Palmer, B., Codling, R., & Mazzoni, S. (1996). Assessing motivation to read. *The Reading Teacher, 49*(7), 518–533.

Guthrie, J. T., & Cox, K. E. (2001). Classroom conditions for motivation and engagement in reading. *Educational Psychology Review, 13*, 283–302.

Jang, H., Reeve, J., & Deci, E. L. (2010). Engaging students in learning activities: It is not autonomy, support or structure but autonomy support and structure. *Journal of Educational Psychology, 102*, 588–600.

Marinak, B., & Gambrell, L. B. (2008). Intrinsic motivation and rewards: What sustains young children's engagement with text? *Literacy Research and Instruction, 47*, 9–26.

Marinak, B., & Gambrell, L. (2009, November 6). *Developmental differences in elementary reading motivation*. Paper presented at the annual meeting of the Association of Literacy Educators and Researchers, Charlotte, NC.

Marinak, B., & Gambrell, L. (2010). Reading motivation: Exploring the elementary gender gap. *Literacy Research and Instruction, 49*(2), 129–141.

McKenna, M., Kear, D. J., & Ellsworth, R. A. (1995). Children's attitudes toward reading: A national survey. *Reading Research Quarterly, 30*, 934–956.

Merisuo-Storm, T. (2006). Girls and boys like to read and write different texts. *Scandinavian Journal of Educational Research, 50*(2), 111–125.

Mohr, K. A. J. (2006). Children's choices for recreational reading: A three-part investigation of selection, preferences, rationales, and processes. *Journal of Literacy Research, 38*(1), 181–104.

Pappas, C. C. (1993). Is narrative "primary"?: Some insights from kindergarteners' pretend readings of stories and informational books. *Journal of Reading Behavior, 25*, 97–129.

Pressley, M., Allington, R. L., Wharton-McDonald, R., Block, C. C., & Morrow, L. M. (2001). *Learning to read: Lessons from exemplary first-grade classrooms*. New York: Guilford Press.

Rettig, M. K., & Hendricks, C. G. (2000). Factors that influence the book selection process of students with special needs. *Journal of Adolescent and Adult Literacy, 43*(7), 608–618.

Skinner, E. A., & Belmont, M. J. (1993). Motivation in the classroom: Reciprocal effects of teacher behavior and students' engagement across the school year. *Journal of Educational Psychology, 85*, 571–581.

Taylor, B. M., Pearson, P. D., Peterson, D. P., & Rodriguez, M. C. (2003). Reading growth in high poverty classrooms: The influence of teacher practices that encourage cognitive engagement in literacy learning. *Elementary School Journal, 104,* 3–28.

Teale, W. H., & Gambrell, L. B. (2007). Raising urban students' literacy achievement by engaging in authentic, challenging work. *The Reading Teacher, 60*(8), 728–739.

Turner, J., & Paris, S. (1995). How literacy tasks influence children's motivation for literacy. *The Reading Teacher, 48*(8), 662–673.

Vygotsky, L. S. (1978). *Mind in society: The development of higher psychological processes.* Cambridge, MA: Harvard University Press.

Zhao, Y. (2009). *Catching up or leading the way: American education in the age of globalization.* Alexandria, VA: Association for Supervision and Curriculum Development.

Index

Page numbers followed by *f* indicate figure, *t* indicate table